Escape From Time

Escape From Time

Disconnecting from Culture

Frederick Kile

Writer's Showcase presented by *Writer's Digest*
San Jose New York Lincoln Shanghai

Escape From Time
Disconnecting from Culture

Published by Writer's Showcase presented by *Writer's Digest*
an imprint of iUniverse.com, Inc.

For information address:
iUniverse.com, Inc.
620 North 48th Street
Suite 201
Lincoln, NE 68504-3467
www.iuniverse.com

ISBN: 0-595-00977-8

Printed in the United States of America

TO YOU–A READER

There are too many "teachers" to thank.
So my thanks goes to you–because you are exploring with me.

From Wisconsin–at the springtime of beginning for
another century–at the NOW of our lives!

I dedicate this book to YOU.

CONTENTS

PART ONE

BACKDROP

Chapter Zero

LOSING TOUCH WITH TIME–AND WITH CULTURE

Americans are immersed in the NOW of life.

The Associated Press reported recently that students in a wealthy town in Massachusetts were suspected of using computer technology to counterfeit U.S. currency. The same technology accelerates change beyond the capacity of institutions to influence personal behavior—not by persuasion and not by coercion.

Did those wealthy students possess advanced technology which they felt immunized them against boundaries set by culture and national institutions?

Or can we say that for those students culture and nation have no meaning?

Culture is part of the past and we don't care about the past. We don't care about the day after tomorrow. We don't like to think about tomorrow—or even about later today.

For many of us, everything we do is short term—and short term might be the next hour—or less.

Together, all of us and all of our actions make up American society. Our society is short-term oriented because *we* are short-term oriented. Or maybe it's the other way around.

What does it mean to us that we think and live in the short term—in the NOW?

How is life changing? How is America changing? Where are we going?

Every society inherits something from the past. Every society inherits music, laws, customs, and stories about famous people. Half of the stories are exaggerations. Most of the other half are sheer fiction. Together, these things from the past are "culture."

American culture is a stew—a mish-mash of immigrant customs, country music, classical and church music, soul music; laws from Europe; legends: George Washington "couldn't tell a lie;" Lincoln "walked a mile to return a penny;" Franklin "flew a kite in a lightning storm to learn about electricity." Some stories are true. We will never know which stories are exaggerations and which are outright fiction.

Leaving the "Old Culture" behind

The last two or three generations have rushed away from our past. Instead of dusting off our past trophies, we move on to win another prize. We think and live as no other society has ever thought or lived—not even our own society before we were born. We live in the short term, and for some of us the short term is "right now." This book uses "NOW" in a special way. "NOW" people are Americans who don't want to focus on anything else but the moment.

The NOW way of life began in America, and it is rapidly spreading beyond America, partly because our TV and films and entertainers are popular almost everywhere and partly because other people also feel tied down by an often irrelevant past.

Thinking about "everywhere" is not practical. If we understand what's happening here in America, we can also think about other countries—if we want to.

Getting rid of the future

Rushing away from our past, we also ignore our future. Our inherited culture assumes a past and a future. We (the people) are society and we have stopped paying attention to our inherited culture. The old culture is "in our way." We pay lip service to the old, dead, irrelevant culture, but we also ignore that culture. The result—our society drifts from one NOW focus to another.

Some questions

"Who thinks about what the Fourth of July means when July 4th actually arrives?" Hardly anybody! Right?

"Who thinks about what Thanksgiving means when 'Turkey Day' comes?" A few people might hear the presidential proclamation read in church on Thanksgiving Day. Have you been to church on Thanksgiving Day, or does the echo of an empty building annoy you?

"Is Christmas a religious holiday in America?"

You get the picture. The old "American way of life" is not how we live. Maybe it was, but not any more.

Gains and losses

We probably wouldn't be the world's leading economy and military power if we held on to the past. We are leaders because we move ahead without any anchors—not even "thought anchors" like, "What might happen if we do something new?" We gain power, money and prestige because we don't hold back.

We don't know what we have lost or what we might lose by living how we live. We don't want to think about "losses." It's not upbeat.

Escape from Time is about us. It's about how we got where we are; about living apart from a culture; about the cost of our choices; about our opportunity to be "bigger than life" or "smaller than life!"

We are unique. The world is watching—and following!

Positive aspects of the NOW orientation

Our society (the way people live) and our inherited customs and institutions are growing farther apart. This is our "social divorce." Our divorce from culture is real—and it is a crisis point.

This crisis is both an opportunity and a threat. The crisis is a threat to life as we know it. It is a threat to social stability. There is a definite risk of societal breakdown.

The crisis offers Americans an opportunity to re-shape or shake off institutional baggage too heavy for a modern society to carry.

If we saw nothing good about an emerging crisis in American life—a crisis defined by a growing gap between how people live and what our inherited institutions expect—we would be saying, "Change is 'bad.'"

Learning

Enormous opportunities arise during societal change. When a society misses these opportunities, it can be damaged for generations.

The French Revolution gave France a chance for a new society but revolutionary leaders did not separate the stellar from the silly. They renamed some months because the old names represented people who didn't fit their idealistic goals. They threw out "July" and "August" because of the connection with Julius and Augustus Caesar. They renamed one summer month "Thermidor"—the "hot one."

Frenchmen were beheaded for resisting absurd changes. In contrast, America focused its revolutionary energy on real change. Clearly, most Americans don't want to honor Julius and Augustus Caesar, but Americans don't even *think* of Julius Caesar when they mention the Fourth of July.

As we shape a new society for a new millennium, our NOW orientation separates us from inherited institutions. We can welcome the separation or we can fight it. We are not about to amplify our social divorce the way the radicals of the French Revolution amplified their societal change. Their "New Society" was gone in ten years. In the vacuum that followed their failure, Napoleon's ruthless march to "glory" killed millions—French youth and other Europeans.

We will lose our opportunity to shape our crisis if we *ignore* it—and we could lose devastatingly if we *resist* the emerging crisis of change.

A final divorce—no going back

American society (the way we live—particularly NOW-oriented people) *is* divorcing our formal culture. Our institutions are outdated. Perhaps a dictatorship could force people to live according to rules from the past. Twice in the 20th century Russia attempted to force its society to live according to worn out institutions. In 1917 the Communists threw out a thousand years of institutional baggage. In 1990, the baggage of Communism brought Russia to its knees again.

France in 1789 and Russia in 1917 and 1990 did not "roll with the punches," and chaos resulted. We will do better.

This book outlines why a crisis is building. We will discuss *some* of the background, but more is happening in our society than one book can discuss. Even if we understood all that is occurring, we *would not be alive long enough* to write the entire story, and if we could, the books would be too massive to read.

Escape from time—is a wakeup call for all Americans. It's better to *wake up while a crisis is brewing* than to read a complete history of the crisis and *why we missed the boat* after our opportunity is gone!

The NOW orientation *is* changing America. Our inherited institutions are *not* relevant to everyday life. This is not a "cookbook" for *the* "right" way to manage the emerging crisis. You readers are the crisis managers, and you will do the right things as the crisis comes into focus for *you* !

Good Managing!

New questions

What is society?

What is culture?

Webster's New World Dictionary-Third College Edition:

Society   "all people, collectively, regarded as constituting a community of related, interdependent individuals."

Culture   "the ideas, customs, skills, arts, etc. of a people or group, that are transferred, communicated or passed along, as in or to succeeding generations."

Our definitions are similar-but we think simpler:

Society—   "The sum total of the actions of people and groups." [What Americans **do** is our society.]

Culture—   "The sum total of inherited beliefs, practices and institutions which guide behavior."

[Religion, philosophy, law, customs, art, tradition; things that *have guided American* society *are* our culture.]

Hard Questions

Why are our prisons overbooked before they are built?

Why did two 16-year olds kill a 22-year old acquaintance in a restaurant in nearby Green Bay, Wisconsin, angry over an argument they had a year before? They had not seen one another during that entire year.

Why are test scores for American high school students so low that tests are re-designed to make students look better than they really are?

Why are people so cynical about our political process? Could it be because some candidates bring aliens to the polls to vote out an incumbent? If a margin of victory is provided by foreigners, what is the meaning of being a citizen? Is it primarily to be eligible for a military draft if a military crisis comes?

Are people cynical because foreign money buys ads to help control our elections? Does this money buy influence? What else does it buy?

Early in the new millennium a six-year old boy shot and killed a first grade girl classmate. Officials campaigned for sympathy for the killer because he was young and "unable to form the intent to kill." A year or two earlier an even younger kindergarten boy kissed a girl classmate on the cheek. Public officials condemned his action and deemed him unfit to be in school. Who can explain the bizarre contrast in the way officials responded to these two events? Or is there no rational explanation?

Do many people ask the questions we just asked?

Does it seem that public leaders haven't a clue about answers to these questions?

Does *anyone* have a clue?

Still more questions

Why does America have hundreds of action groups, thousands of "fix-it" groups, and yet new problems are uncovered every day? Will TV newscasts ever run out of nasty social problems to "expose?"

When newscasts and magazines and newspapers point to "causes" for American social problems, are those "causes" part of a chain of symptoms beginning with a larger social or cultural illness…symptoms of a dislocation which changed how society and culture fit together?

What does it mean that our society is divorcing our culture?

In this "social divorce," who suffers most? Don't children usually suffer most from a divorce?

Understanding ourselves

There are many unanswerable questions because we don't know who we are. This book is written to help us know ourselves.

Time

—*and* this book is about **time**. Time has many meanings. Time is an important measure of how things relate to each other. Time is also a scientific measure, but this book is concerned with time as a benchmark to measure how society and culture interact.

Many people have escaped from time and do not want time as a measure in their lives. They want to measure each moment, each impulse, by itself—or, as a friend (a parish pastor from Philadelphia) says, "People do what they want. They are only 'wrong' when they are caught." People detach their actions from time. Each moment (except the moment they are 'caught' by a cultural institution), they act by impulse, detached from time and from the inherited institutions of a dying culture—institutions which serve themselves by using time to tie people to a culture they do not want.

One more set of serious questions

Why is there a divorce between
  A. Our society (all of us comprise our society) and
  B. Our formal culture (customs and moral and behavioral norms inherited from prior generations and the institutions which manage how these norms are applied in everyday life)?

What will happen to our society and our culture when we recognize that this social divorce is irreconcilable?

Some consequences of the social divorce

America spends more on education than any other country. We have greater access to computers than any other people. The possible monetary career rewards for an education are unmatched anywhere else.

In spite of these factors, one major result of the growing gap between American people and their culture is a decline of educational achievement. A close friend teaches graduate level quantum mechanics at a large state university. Over half of his students are from other countries, some of them from so-called "developing countries." What does this say about our educational achievements? The friend will soon retire. Will the next professor be from somewhere else?

There is a pattern of social change which *is* American life. This change has been unfolding for decades. No segment of our society caused this pattern of change but every sector of our society contributed to how we changed. There is no "credit" and no "blame" any more than one could "blame" or "credit" someone because railroads connected East with West in this country in the 1800s. Change is unavoidable. We are not able even to imagine a world without change.

How will America cope with this pattern of change? Will we cope successfully?

Some of the answers are in this book. Most of the answers are in what you—and the rest of us—do!

Chapter One

Continuous Time

According to one survey, growing numbers of people now think that their best chance of having a prosperous retirement is by purchasing lottery tickets. The survey was unnecessary. We can see what people do.

Contrast the "lottery ticket mentality" with the traditional American outlook, "Save and invest and you will have enough money to enjoy retirement." The "traditional" outlook assumed continuity in life—what we do today affects our lives at a later time called "the future."

"The future" seemed real to people who experienced time as a continuous flow. They believed that what happened in the past influenced what happens today and that their decisions in the present will affect what happens in the future.

This was America's orientation toward time—life is lived in the flow of a moving stream we call time.

The idea that people experience time as continuous is still believed intellectually, but *psychologically* Americans live outside of time in a world of NOW. Intellectual "knowledge" does not imply psychological acceptance. People behave as though there are no future consequences to what they do—not because they don't understand consequences—not because they don't believe statistics, but because they don't connect psychologically with time as continuous. Smoking, promiscuous unprotected sex, driving while impaired are not psychologically connected with something that lies ahead because there is no conviction that *anything* is ahead.

America was built on expectations of something better ahead. For some Americans the future was not even expected in their lifetime. It didn't matter because their children and grandchildren would experience the results of what those people did.

Our Constitution was written for others much more than for the people who signed it. Jefferson paid an "outrageous" sum to Napoleon to buy Louisiana and a huge chunk of the middle of North America. He wasn't going to live there, but his country would need it.

Horace Greeley's famous quote, "Go West, young man, go West," was meant to lead the young men and the women who went with them to a better future.

Millions of illiterates came to America from Europe and immediately sent their children to school.

Those people believed that tomorrow would be built on today—and they lived that way.

Gradually, the psychological meaning of a future was compressed into shorter and shorter time spans, and then, in the 20th century, Americans began to lose touch—first with the past and then with the future. They escaped from time—without knowing what was happening. Continuous time was reduced from a psychological home for living to a psychological fiction without real meaning.

When we look back at the fuzzy image of that psychological world of continuous time, we are uncomfortable with what we see—because we are different than they were. We realize that we would not be at home in their world.

If we make a serious attempt to study the era of Continuous Time, what do we see? The "good old days" of Continuous Time left more problems than joys—debts from someone else's loans, hangovers from other people's parties which we didn't attend. They may have had good reasons for what they did while they began to hurry through time, but we can't internalize their thinking. Consider what we inherited: a mountainous federal debt; a welfare system that generates dependency and destroys self-respect for its clients; huge stockpiles of nuclear weapons, poison gases, and bio-weapons piled up before most of us were born, power plants with tons of radioactive waste that we can't store and can't get rid of.

You might just want to get away from all this. Why do you want to pay off inherited debts or recover from someone else's hangover?

No one should be surprised that younger people prefer not to "own" the past, not to think about the future. Consider the outlook for them:

+ Decreasing personal safety—how many cell phones are bought just for safety?
+ Decreasing job security—plenty of jobs, most of them under the banner "The future is now."
+ Increasing social stratification—"You are what you earn." And income distribution is changing.

Continuity in life morphs into something new—"everything is up for grabs."

Time and continuity were put up for grabs during an era of *analysis*.

Chapter Two

ANALYTICAL TIME

The erosion of continuous time—during an era of analysis

The average American might still think of time as continuous—one minute follows another and minutes become hours and days and years. That same American does not experience time as continuous.

Most of us experience time pressure. Time pressure is a *symptom* of forces that re-oriented our American view of time away from awareness of past, present, and future (continuous time) toward analyzing what might happen and what did happen.

In the business world, management's goal is to control the corporate future. To accomplish this, staffs of professionals are assigned to analyze. Some people gather data; other people analyze the same data every which way, and managers read and digest reports based on these analyses. This penchant for analysis has profound consequences.

What happened?

Especially for people under age 40—"time" is over. Past, present, future simply don't exist. There *was* a past and a future. Events *were* connected. Two or three generations of people living by analysis broke the continuity and chewed up the present. How did this happen?

Analytical people are paid to critique and analyze what has occurred and to forecast what is likely to happen. For several decades, analytically-minded people in analytical jobs used the present as a "vantage point" for analysis, not a "moment for living." The easy flow of time through three phases of past present and future was separated into two disconnected halves.

> One "half of time" contains *what has already occurred*; analysts milk every bit of data and information from events and numbers; what was once "the past" has become something to be measured;
> The second "half of time" contains *what will happen*. What will happen "needs" to be forecast so managers can maximize control of coming events.

For analysts and their managers, the present tense of life is only an interlude between past and future. This interlude has little meaning by itself—except as a platform from which to analyze and forecast.

Analysis separates the past from the lives of the analysts as they examine it. The driving questions are: "Has the past measured up to what we anticipated? Did the actual past produce the results which were forecasted?" The analysts examine the past apart from life as they experienced it. Then they create new expectations, new forecasts based on newly selected data. These new forecasts are carefully separated from how analysts might experience life. This "sanitary approach" to data and forecasts centers on an effort to keep the work of the analysts from intersecting with their lives. This eliminates "researcher bias."

Analytical society is all around us, grinding away—studying markets, downsizing to impress Wall Street, re-engineering, and promoting lifestyles which meet corporate needs. An irritating byproduct of the hurricane of analysis is a jungle of new terminology with a three year life expectancy—in its first year, a term is trendy; the next year it's used by everybody; the third year it's like yesterday's coffee. In one company I worked for, a team of analysts spent days creating the acronym

HERMANN (Heuristic Error Rejecting Monitor Achieving Noise Negation) to describe a complex piece of electronic equipment.

Witty names like HERMANN and other terminology with a short life span are part of a jargon fog we live in. The fog is thickened by unintelligible professional language. The jargon fog and the professional language are unrelated to our lives.

Consider an example of fog: "This property will probably be included in the estate of a transferor, under Sec. 2036(a) of the Internal Revenue Code, if he or she continues to occupy or use the property without paying reasonable compensation to the partnership." [Translation: "Your estate will be taxed when you die, if you use partnership property without paying for it."]

The analytical jungle and its partner, professional jargon fog, represent an approach to work which alienates Americans from their own lives. We have made corporate life in America impossible unless we have squads of analysts creating reports and reading other people's reports.

We lose touch with our own lives when we spend our days and years forecasting what might happen and analyzing what did happen.

The analytical dynasty

An era of analysis began accelerating about fifty or sixty years ago. Maybe it began even earlier with Taylor's studies of lighting in an industrial setting. The Second World War pushed national leaders to analyze coded messages, local newspapers from Europe, radio broadcasts, terrain and weather in battle areas, aerial photos. It's hard to imagine where all the analysts came from. When the post-war economy soared, finely-tuned wartime analytical skills were focused on products and profit. Analysis ruled a new economy. With the climate change from war to peace, analysts—almost like frogs—changed form along the way. They began with slide rules and big books of tables, and a generation later analysts were staring at computer screens. Analysts focused on a growing array of computer-based tools. Spreadsheets substituted for real life.

The analysts gave birth to the analytical society which is all around us, grinding away—studying markets and organizations, downsizing, upsizing, re-engineering, and promoting lifestyles to conform with someone's idea of what will meet their company's marketing plan needs.

Analysts create an artificial world, describing events in detail before they occur. They anticipate a future which cannot materialize. Randomness guarantees that their forecasts will be wrong. When a forecast is wrong, teams of analysts explain why it was wrong, and the rest of us analyze what these analysts said.

There is always more data to analyze (summaries of summaries), so analysts increasingly work by exception. If what occurred was *expected*, it is discarded as "uninteresting." If what occurred was *unexpected*, it is analyzed and sliced into tiny pieces for further analysis. Life is not experienced in a time frame which is contemporary with what is being analyzed.

When analysis dominates living, what has happened is forgotten faster and faster. What is approaching comes faster and faster. To deal with this speed, analysts sharpen their skills of observation and accelerate their analysis, developing a kind of "warp perception."

What is warp perception?

Warp perception is a psychological compression of past, present, and future into perceiving life in only two modes. [Time itself does not come in "modes." "Modes of time" is a convenient shorthand expression for "ways of relating to time."] Life is perceived according to:

1. What is approaching
2. What has occurred

Analysts spend so much mental energy on looking ahead and looking back that the Continuous Time categories of past, present, and future lose significance. "Time" is split into two discontinuous modes—past and future, with a discontinuity separating the two.

In the process, analysts surrender a sense of the past. A former mayor of my city, Appleton, Wisconsin, said, "Americans throw away the past."

When the concept of past had meaning, the "past" was something to learn from. People or events "lived again," though objectively they were gone. History had dry and dusty aspects, but history was populated by real people whose lives said something about living in the present. Mistakes of history guided some people—some leaders—to watch for gaps in their thinking.

Past and future as games

For analysts, the past as something with meaning for today is gone. Instead, we believe that events occurred so we can analyze them. The past is a "game" that can be replayed—and maybe we can "fix" it. As analysts, we evaluate events—subconsciously expecting that people and events might come around *a second time and this time they* (the people and events being analyzed) will listen to *us*, the analysts.

The future is also unreal. As analysts, we believe the future should listen to us and follow our advice. "If it were *really* going to happen, the future would not lurk 'out there' somewhere. It would make itself the context for our analysis."

Like the smoke of a nearly dead fire, the idea of a future is gone. When the elder Mayor Richard Daley of Chicago said, "I have a great nostalgia for the future," he did not know how prophetic he was.

The analytical desert

Everyone is psychologically tuned to a dominant time mode. My childhood was spend in the context of Continuous Time, but I later worked in an analytical world. I worked and lived in Analytical Time for years but gradually realized I was wandering through a psychological desert. People around me seemed alive and I felt sort of "on a shelf," like a dusty, discarded computer. This slow realization became a wakeup call.

Millions of Americans, especially those who are between 40 and 55 at the beginning of the new millennium are analysts—especially people who read a lot. Many leave too little room for life, too little room for experience. There are exceptions—violent, or powerful moments; compelling, painful, or overwhelming events. The nature of the exceptions evokes a psychological hunger for life. But life easily eludes the analyzing person.

Analysis is a national obsession. People who don't relate to stocks analyze soap operas, or football drafts or game plans and postgame analysis of key plays. They analyze TV coverage of a terrorist attack or a murder. Our love affair with analysis explains America's multi-year fixation on the murders of Nicole Brown Simpson and Ronald Goldman and the ensuing trial of O.J. Simpson. And it explains our fascination with the pathetic murder of six-year-old Jon Benet Ramsey.

Analysts become exhausted from frequent re-interpretation—one time pessimistic, the next optimistic. Eventually they become almost fully detached from their own lives. Events cannot compete with their buildups and replays.

Through ceaseless anticipation and analysis of what is coming and what happened yesterday, analysis devalues the present. The way is prepared for a complete escape from time.

Time as irrelevant—the NOW orientation

Three different views of time exist in America: Continuous Time, Analytical Time, and NOW. In Continuous Time, people see life as a continuous flow, and they believe that events have consequences. When the future arrives, they look back in time and see how "yesterday" shaped "today." They are convinced that "today's" events will affect "tomorrow."

When people are lost, they look for something new. Many analysts do not recognize what they miss by living in their time mode, but people around them do—especially their children. Analytical Time was empty, barren and directionless. It gave way to a new mode of time—Escape From Time—what we call NOW.

For young people it's impossible to construct an experience of time as continuous. They can't "go back" to what they never knew psychologically. The concept of a past related to a living present or a living present related to a real future is useless theory to them. But younger people do sense something which is alive—the NOW orientation of many other young people. By running away from analysis or another emptiness in life, they feel the power of impulse and get into NOW. To them, this is living!

Irrelevant institutions

National institutions are the formal structures of our culture. They operate like relics of a fairy-tale past.

Our institutions assume that we had a past and will have a future—and even worse—these cultural relics try to force us to claim an unwanted past, a dubious future.

Many institutions feel like another headache from somebody's "good old days." Example: during the1980s there were still government programs for widows of veterans of the Civil War. A few of the oldest Civil War veterans married much younger women and a handful of those women were still living in the 1980s. Could anyone calculate the overhead costs of providing a few benefit dollars to these "sufferers" from the American Civil War? Is it any wonder that people don't care even to *hear* about the past?

Time is like a fairy tale to us at the beginning of a new millennium— a fairy tale like the Old West or like a Sitcom. We all somehow know that the Old West was never really like what we see on TV and that sitcoms are unreal. Westerns and sitcoms are fairy tales to help us escape from thinking about anything.

We have gradually come to feel the same way about time. We escape from time to escape from thinking deeply about anything. There is only this moment—no past—no tomorrow.

All we have is NOW. NOW frees us from the past. We have put the past where it belongs—on library shelves—out of sight, out of mind. We don't care about the past—and why should we?

This book is about NOW—about how we live, how we act, how we fit together as a society (or do *not* fit together). And this book is about how we escaped from the traditional, continuous sense of time—past, present, future—how we escaped to NOW. For NOW people, only *this moment* counts. Live by impulse—no roots, no anchors, no restraints.

Society clashes with culture

The emptiness of analysis, the burden of outdated institutions, opened the door for NOW, for living by IMPULSE. In the NOW life, America's people clash with America's "culture," with ossified formal institutions from another era. Institutions cannot evolve fast enough. Our fast-moving society will toss institutions aside and create something new. Transitions from one set of institutions to another may sound smooth and "natural" on the pages of a history book, but societal transitions lead to major dislocations and suffering. People lose control of their lives at the same time the institutions which they depend on for structure and stability are crumbling. Societal trauma follows a clash between people's behavior and institutions. Occasionally, a revolution sweeps away old institutions and chaos follows. In our present circumstances we are more likely to experience "institutional exhaustion" as society gropes for new institutions—for a *new culture*.

Institutions become exhausted when they cannot cope with their own problems. Consider a fourth-grade teacher with several challenged students, including a girl who cannot focus on what is being taught unless the teacher keeps her hand on the girl's shoulder. This woman teaches virtually the entire day, every day, from the side of her classroom, with her comforting hand on the girl's shoulder to help the girl learn something and to keep her from totally disrupting the class. The teacher is exhausted and frustrated and will leave her career. The principal of the school will be frustrated to her limits when this excellent teacher leaves. This is a prescription for expanding personal exhaustion to institutional exhaustion.

NOW people act on impulse. They see "morality" as a meaningless heritage from someone else and *for* someone else. They live without acknowledging consequences of actions because their psychological orientation is apart from context. NOW actions have no context—but consequences *are* contextual. Our cultural institutions are foreign to NOW people because the institutions view actions in the context of continuous time—past, present, future.

Analysts and NOW people pass like ships in the night, unable to see each other and blind to institutions based on an irrelevant view of time.

A societal divorce is occurring

While analysts study the past, compute imaginary futures, and develop new statistical techniques, the "present" disappears for them. They think about what *did* happen and what *might* happen. "Living" is postponed indefinitely. One young couple began living together in the early 1980s. After successfully sharing their lives for several years, they planned a wedding, which they *postponed* at the last minute. Nearly every year since—almost twenty years that they have lived together—the mother of the woman asks the parents of the man, "What do you suppose 'postpone' means?" The couple adjusted because the adjustment is within their time orientation—whatever their idea of a moral orientation.

The same adjustment is impossible for the parents. They cannot adjust to a time paradigm outside of their psychological thought world.

They accept the next generation, but they don't understand their reasoning patterns. The not-so-young-anymore couple moved beyond the analytical world of no time for the present to a new world of impulse. If they ever do marry, it will be driven by impulse.

Is America alone in experiencing a clash between culture and people? Probably not, but the clash between formal culture and the people's relationship to time is more intense in the U.S. The U.S. is the seed bed for this clash.

Because this time clash developed in America, American culture has begun to adapt to its people. America's cultural institutions are changing. But they are changing slowly, much more slowly than the people are changing.

The people are not waiting for the culture to change. Social change is outrunning institutional change, and no one can be sure of what will happen when the residual bond between the people and their institutions disappears completely. Consider the young girl who needs the teacher's hand to calm her sufficiently to make it through the day. Family dynamics and political pressures have transferred responsibility for many young people like that girl from the family to the schools—long before the schools could prepare for rapid change. There is an inherent delay of ten years from the introduction of new demands on a school system until teachers with new skills are trained and enter the teaching profession in large numbers. During the long delay, many experienced teachers leave because they can no longer cope with fluid work demands, and the wait for trained and experienced teachers becomes still longer. This is one example of how social change outpaces the ability of institutions to change. During these periods of change, the support base for institutions erodes and society loses faith in its institutions.

The residual bond between people and institutions is weakening in many other areas. The U.S. military decided to immunize personnel against anthrax—a deadly disease. However, there were no broadly-based studies of the effects of the vaccine, so many military personnel refused the vaccine. A long-standing bond between the military command and its constituency both within the armed forces and in the civilian population was severely strained over this issue, a result of rapid change in the larger environment.

Chapter Three

HALF-ALIVE IN ANALYTICAL TIME

From stodgy to loose cannons in one generation

People might adapt on occasion to different time orientations, but psychologically life is best in one time orientation. Once an analyst (and perhaps still one) I find myself longing to become a NOW person. I grew up in the wake of the Great Depression and World War II, so my original time orientation was Continuous Time. My academic training and the Zeitgeist gradually turned me into an analyst. It's not easy to "go backward" from being an analyst to living in Continuous Time, but the loneliness of analysis makes life in the analytical desert almost unbearable—especially for people who lived part of their lives outside the analytical desert. Looking for life beyond the barren analytical desert, it is possible to discover NOW living, but even when it is discovered, NOW living is not completely comfortable for someone whose original psychological home was in another time orientation. As much as anything, the lack of a psychological home in a single time orientation forced me to begin sifting through how we relate to time.

Society today is led by three different groups of people. Analysts form two of these leadership groups. The other group of leaders are emerging NOW people.

First, there are analysts who pretend to pay attention to the past and the future. Analytical leaders, particularly politicians, try to straddle the chasm between Continuous Time and Analytical Time. Politicians rely on their own analytical skills and the work of staff analysts and try to present believable "solutions" to economic and social issues. At the same time, politicians seek to appeal to voters, but tens of millions of voters live and think in terms of Continuous Time—especially older voters.

As politicians and other analytical leaders move between two time orientations, they seem to be vacillating. This apparent vacillation is perceived as weakness and insincerity, especially by their opponents. The public senses that something is "wrong," and dismisses large numbers of politicians and leaders lightly—and calls them insincere. The problem is compounded because analytical politicians and leaders work to understand the world around them, especially the factors which attract voters, but they do not understand themselves. They do not understand that they are trying to live in two different thought worlds. They do not understand who they really are, and this lack of self understanding amplifies their aura of insincerity. It is irrelevant whether a leader or politician really *is* sincere. The aura of insincerity is a product of dissonance within the leader's self. This aura of insincerity ballooned even more during the 1998 state elections in Minnesota, and a third group—buttressed by many NOW people and young analysts for whom Continuous Time is meaningless—stepped into the gap and elected a true political maverick, Jesse Ventura, as governor.

Second, a smaller group of analysts are the technocrats and the "nerds" who gave us the cyberworld. They have no room for the present, no room for experience. There are exceptions—erotic, violent, or powerful moments; compelling, painful, or overwhelming events. The very nature of the exceptions evokes a hunger for the moment, a hunger for life. Even in these moments, hard-core analysts are psychologically unable to live life to its fullest. They compensate in ways which help them seem to have full lives. At the edges of society there are analytical people who really are dangerous—to people around them, to themselves, and to society as a whole. Consider the mysteries surrounding the Unabomber—letter bombs killing or maiming carefully targeted and widely scattered victims.

Third, some leaders are NOW people. They have escaped from continuity and they live by impulse. They create, and they live without future accountability. These two characteristics, creativity and freedom from accountability, free them from limits. The most creative NOW people are geniuses taking society where it has never been. This group "made the difference" in the Minnesota state elections in 1998.

A few in this third group are "loose cannons," rolling here and there across the deck of the wildly pitching ship we call society, bringing with them the dangers sailors once associated with cannons loose on the deck of their ship, but the few "loose cannons" are not the mainstream of this emerging group of leaders.

The birth of NOW

Two generations of analysts worked and existed in the analytical desert for all but their most powerful emotional experiences, which were limited to brief segments of clock time. With a fixed gaze staring at data and results, these analysts gave birth to "warp perception"—grasping and processing as much "information" as possible at an ultimately unsustainable pace.

In the crush to understand, some people felt an intense desire to escape the bonds of analysis and to experience life, but most of them did not escape the analytical desert. The *next* generation recognized the gaping emptiness of analytical life and said, "We want a life, and we want it NOW."

The NOW generation (already in its second biological generation and drawing in a third biological generation) recognized how far their analytical parents and grandparents were from the "old" America around them—the inherited culture, which was built on a foundation of continuous time. Parents and grandparents lived in a vacuum—far apart from their own lives and unable to relate to the "old" context.

Reacting to empty lives

Children and grandchildren of analysts observed the barrenness of the analytical desert, but they could not "go back" to what was already disappearing—Continuous Time. They escaped all prior conceptions of time and chose NOW. The NOW generation was born.

Waking up

My personal wakeup call came from watching football. After years of following Green Bay Packer football on television, I began attending games in person. How I got the tickets is still a mystery to many people around me because the stadium has been sold out for forty years. My policy regarding the tickets is, "Don't ask, don't tell."

The contrast between sitting in the stadium and watching a game on television made it seem like two different sports.

When I'm there in person, I am involved. Even though I'm only a spectator, I participate. The home team wants crowd noise for a crucial defensive play, quiet for key plays when they have the ball. The team responds to what the fans do—to what I do. In a small way, I am part of the game. Sixty thousand people are part of the game. For the millions who watch a game on television, it's an entirely different experience. A borderline call is critiqued by the broadcasters, reviewed and re-reviewed until the flow of action is lost for the TV viewer. A few freeze-frames determine what people think of a play.

When I'm in the stadium, I'm aware that a particular play only happens once. Events flow on. Contrast that with what fans watch at home. At home, we see the same play over and over again. The flow is gone. At home we anticipate and analyze but don't really experience what is going on. Instead of being involved, we are analysts.

When I stay home, I trade the enjoyment of a real happening for closeups of what *seems* like accuracy, but in truth the medium is the message. The television viewer does not have the option of looking "over there" at something else going on in the stadium or of keeping an eye on a favorite player. The viewer sees only what the video editor puts on the screen.

As part of the crowd experiencing a game, I don't have time to analyze every foot movement and every strange bounce of the ball. At the end, I leave with an impression of what happened—real people did real things and then the game ended. In this way, I re-connect with life; I see that on videotape a moment, or a play or the entire game may never end. As television audience we view "managed reality," but the actual game is played "one-time-through."

Video replays of a game fade away only after a long series—sometimes weeks—of "what if" questions, but meanwhile, the game itself ends. The teams and the coaches move on and prepare for the next game.

This distinction is real to NOW people. They want to *be* the action. They want to participate in the game. The game is a moment in NOW life.

Getting from there to here

The story of how our society changed is first and foremost the story of a journey through the emptiness of analysis.

What is "there" and what is "here?" "There" is the "good old days"—an era which had a past, and had a future, an era which felt like part of that past or that future. That era is gone. Along the way, we became a nation of analysts—when we tire of analysis, we move another step—out of the flow of time completely. It's not that clock and calendar stop. When we escape time, we no longer pay attention to the movement of the clock and of the calendar. No matter how much hype there is about a change of date or year, we choose to live in the moment. We choose impulse—We choose NOW.

By becoming a nation of analysts, did we also become a nation of scholars? Hardly.

Analysts dissect everything from the trivial to the unusual. Forecasts and evaluations involve serious subjects and playful subjects: stock markets, horoscopes, soap operas, horse racing, crime, election results.

Once upon a time—there *was* a past, a future. There was even a present time, connected to that past and to that future.

We can barely remember that "once upon a time." It was shredded by an analytical society.

Analytical society is the society of American business and media. It grinds away—studying markets and organizations, downsizing, upsizing, re-engineering, and promoting a bouquet of lifestyles to conform with someone's analysis of what meets their industry's needs. Out of their analyses, experts and marketers create a jungle of hype and of trendy terminology, and we exist in that jungle.

The analysts—who are they? They are *us. We* are analysts. We swallow up the present time thinking about what *did* happen and what *might* happen. (It hardly ever happens that way, anyhow!)

Life is spent analyzing instead of living.

Analysis creates an artificial world. Events and actions are described in detail *before* they occur.

In this way, we anticipate a future which *cannot* materialize according to the forecasts. Randomness in the world *guarantees* that forecasts *will be* wrong.

When a forecast is (almost inevitably) wrong, an army of *analysts* work to explain why it was wrong, and the rest of us analyze what these analysts said.

A note on analysis

Do not mistake our description of the origins of NOW. We have not condemned analysis. Analysis provides society with wonderful benefits.

We have described the behavior of two or three generations of people who overused a set of intellectual tools until these tools dominated their lives. The reaction to the overuse of analysis and to the economic prosperity it fostered contributed to the birth of NOW society.

Exhaustion

We are exhausted from interpretation—one interpretation is pessimistic, another optimistic.

Finally, we detach from our own lives. Events cannot compete with their buildup and their own replays.

Separating from our institutions

Our cultural institutions were created when life was a lived as a progression from "a past, to a present, and into a future."

"Analytical time" detached "present" from past and future. Americans escaped from time. As a result, we do not understand our institutions—and we do not understand our culture. We are capable of analyzing our institutions, but we do not live in them. They are foreign to us.

Institutions feel like strange intrusions from another culture. In fact, our institutions ARE intruders from another culture. That culture is gone, but it seems to dominate us through leftover institutions.

In part we cannot change our institutions or our social structure because our mechanisms for change are also leftovers from another culture.

Consider our two large political parties. Every few years we hear how one party or the other is "ready to die." In reality, each party owes large debts to a few pressure groups committed to narrow agendas. These groups are far from acknowledging that we live in a new America. In strange combinations, these various pressure groups keep the two outmoded political parties alive.

Pressure groups are a life support system for moribund parties which ought to have died. It's like keeping the body of a nearly dead person going until a decision is made on how to parcel out his or her assets.

An example from elsewhere: when Marshall Tito, the long-time dictator of Yugoslavia died, life support systems kept his body functioning for several days after life had disappeared—while would-be successors parceled out political power. They could not "afford" to let Tito "die" (though he really was dead) until their moribund structures were artificially propped up.

Something similar happened in Spain when Franco died. Teams of physicians worked to keep a half-conscious Franco going while factions positioned themselves for post-Franco power. The Generalissimo said, "Gad, it's hard to die!"

Our cultural institutions are changing to move to where the people are, but institutions do not change very quickly. By design they cannot change rapidly—they change only through slow processes like constitutional amendments or the death of old institutions and the birth of new ones.

Old institutions are often wealthy and powerful and they die reluctantly. We have corporations which "should" have died long ago but were wealthy enough to live beyond their useful life.

Other corporations appear to have survived, but have really been re-born over a long time. It is as though a corporation died and was re-born in another lifetime. Example: the Ford Motor Company of today barely resembles the Ford of the 1930s. The Ford Motor Company nearly died in the 1940s, and it went through years of rebuilding before re-emerging very different from what it was when Henry Ford was living.

"Analytical time" is only a way station on the path to "NOW" time. In the 21st century Americans live in NOW time—apart from the flow of events which characterized the "old-fashioned" America.

A classic film, "My Dinner with Andre," described an all-night dinner with Andre. The most striking moment of the movie came when it was dawn and Andre was suddenly gone and all that remained for the other guest (the guest was essentially a prop for Andre) was a memory of the all-night monologue by Andre. The monologue was almost continuous—and then, suddenly, it was over. The "conversation/monologue" was isolated from what went before and what came after. The conversation was similar to a microcosm of analytical life. Andre really lived and then lived his life another time in the dinner conversation, but the guest was only a spectator. He listened to life without living it.

Chapter 4

ESCAPE FROM TIME

Isolated time

Beyond analytical time—there is *another* experience of time. Separate a single instant of time from the rest of time and live only in that instant. Call the instant "NOW," and ignore what used to be called the past and the future. The instant is isolated from the rest of time.

This isolated moment is NOW. To live in NOW is to *escape from time*.

For NOW people the moment, the instant, is detached from everything else.

This isolated instant called NOW, is not the same as the "present" of traditional time. The old "present" was connected to the rest of time. NOW is not connected to anything else on the timeline.

Isolated time is NOW

NOW is not the same as the "objective" present of analytical time [NOW is not utilized to analyze anything], and NOW is certainly not the traditional "present" because a NOW person doesn't care if time is continuous or not. A NOW person is psychologically apart from the passage of time in a continuous flow. NOW thinking does not disdain the flow of time any more than we disdain the theory of relativity in our everyday lives, which we live without a thought about relativity.

What the NOW person does is simply what he/she does, period— apart from any consideration of an artificial connection with an artificial past or future. Life is lived NOW, not as part of "time."

Analysis is like a detached hobby for NOW people. Perhaps NOW people do analyze something which happened or might happen, but they don't really *connect* with it. They are just having mental fun.

A new way of thinking about time

In its youth, our culture learned to think about time in terms of "past, present, and future."

These three aspects of time…past, present, future…perhaps they are simply psychological constructs. No one really knows the nature of time. Is time linear? Is it a series of things that happen one after another? Is time a series of events with gaps in between? Has everything already been planned and people are just living out a script…like performing an ancient play? Is everything happening at once, but we perceive things in some sequence?

These questions are important to philosophers, but we are not searching for a philosophy of time.

We simply want to know—How does our attitude toward time affect our lives? We want to understand how our lives are shaped by the way we perceive time.

Orphaned from our culture

We *do* confront an issue—the way we perceive time separates us from our cultural institutions and our inherited moral norms. We no longer accept the broad mix of written and inherited traditions which once shaped behavior. Our formal culture no longer represents us. We are cultural orphans.

We escaped from time—to live in NOW, isolated from any past or future. Are we aliens in our own culture, not merely orphans?

A sudden shift from analysis to NOW

Time is a hindrance to action. We do not want to think about what happened before and we certainly do not want to let a vague, uncertain future influence what we do, so we escape from time. NOW is its own past and future. Only what happens NOW matters at all.

NOW is all that remains of traditional time after it is stripped of meaning by impersonal analysis of almost everything. Analysis removed the sense of reality from life. NOW living has a sense of reality.

The new "time orientation" is NOW. NOW people live for whatever they are doing "right now." If there is a "now generation," it is composed of people who have lost touch with past and future, some by choice, others because they do not know anything else.

Without past and future, people act out feelings of the moment. What NOW people do has no antecedents and no consequences. Doing is driven by impulse, the feeling of the NOW moment. Impulse living *resembles* living in the "old-fashioned" present of "continuous" time, but impulse living is really living by conditioning.

Prevailing trends condition a NOW person to act. Trends *instruct* the NOW person how to act. One trend of the new century is the increasing acceptance of individual violence.

A passenger who has no cab fare murders a cab driver.

A person who wants to see someone die kills another person

A teen-ager who wants a jacket murders whoever is wearing it and takes the jacket.

A high-schooler who wants some shoes, kills another student to take his shoes.

A worker who dislikes a boss kills as many co-workers as possible.

A student who is shunned shoots his classmates and plans
to blow up the school.

These are NOW acts with a powerful thrust of violence.

The earliest NOW actions did not make strong "statements" involving murder. The trend toward violent "statements"—often climaxing in
killing—is NOW behavior in full bloom.

To people still oriented toward traditional time, this sort of violence
seems random and cruel.

For analysts, people who anticipate and who evaluate—violent
"statements" are statistics.

For NOW people the impulse to "wear the jacket" or "wear the
shoes" or "get revenge" drives a killing. Impulse triggers an act. There is
no "past" to guide the action in some way. Justification is not needed
because there is no future to consider. After an action, the mood is…"I
felt like it."

That another person is dead is not an issue…the dead person never
"was" because nothing "was." There is no past. Punishment is irrational
because acting in the NOW is not punishable. Acting NOW is simply
what we *do*. We expect a feeling, and we do what we must to get that
feeling. Moral judgments do not apply.

When an act has no consequences, the act itself is its only reward. If
unpleasant consequences flow to the person who acts, life is "unfair."

Life is a casino

Life is a casino. In the casino, we pull the handle on a slot machine—
something happens. Suspense lasts for an instant. We create each event
separately and it lasts for a second or maybe two.

Really, hardly anyone pulls a handle in the casino. The slots have
been "improved" to give us more instants of NOW. As long as "credit"
remains on the machine, we push a lighted button which says "spin
reels" This helps us dive deeper into NOW time, helps us detach further

from anything else. NOW time is king in the casino. NOW time is the ONLY time in the casino.

Politicians and social workers say they are concerned about "gambling addiction," about drug and alcohol addiction, about addiction to sex or addiction to crime, and perhaps they "should" be concerned.

Politicians and social workers are "analysts" who focus their worries on specific addictions, but their own lives are discontinuous. Many of these people are buried in analysis, and ignore what has happened to the perception of time in America.

NOW, by its very nature, does not consider anything beyond the immediate impulse which triggers an action. The impulse triggering an action is not "considered." The impulse is just a trigger, nothing more.

The casino is the fountain of the "moment." Each moment springs from nothing else, like a fireworks display. The naive child in each person sees each burst of fireworks without thinking about the person launching the rocket, without considering the sweat shop that built the rocket, without thinking about medieval Chinese chemists who invented fireworks. Each starburst is unique and alone, without antecedent or consequent.

Likewise in the casino. Each deal of a card in a blackjack game is unique, a moment by itself. If the occasional "card counter" tries to make it otherwise, he/she is soon "schooled" in living for the moment by a casino strongarm or given a mafia style lecture on being "nice." The shrewd learn from the lecture. The rest are fitted with more permanent clothing.

Quickie life—and death

But people don't live only in casinos. They don't play only in casinos. Let's visit a recent Los Angeles awards party for rock musicians. A guest, a visiting musician, is pushed to the floor. Maybe he says something or looks strangely at someone. Maybe he looks different from everyone else. He is stomped and kicked to death by a group of partygoers near him. They have not pre-planned anything. They never met him before. They haven't planned to murder him. The pushing and stomping are impulse actions.

Those of us not at the party can ask, "Was this murder at all?" Or—more pointedly—"Was this a crime?"

Old fashioned cultural institutions and social norms ask those questions and expect "Yes" answers. NOW people expect totally different answers.

To whom does our culture belong?

Does our culture belong to an amorphous aggregation of people now dead? To an almost equally amorphous aggregation of people now living? If this culture belongs to the latter group, perhaps it is because this group is still alive and is still evolving. The aggregation of forefathers (foremothers?) now dead may have been great people, but however great, they can no longer grow and evolve.

Consider the stomping in LA as the NOW generation participants see it. In the NOW view this action has no historical antecedents to shape it because there is no "past." Neither does this action have any consequences—because there is no "future" to consider.

A decision to act or not to act is based on impulse. Whatever seems appealing is a likely choice. If two or more actions can be chosen, the momentary mood of the actor determines the action.

Our escape from time isolates us from the possibility of continuity and it separates us from whatever meaning analysis might once have had.

We are simply part of NOW!

PART TWO

CHANGE

Chapter Five

NOW Emerges

The American *Escape from Time* straddles three "generations:"

Traditional people—comfortable in the past-present-future world of continuous time;

Analytical people—sacrifice the present to looking backward and forward in time. By looking backward and forward, they break the continuity of time and lose touch with their own lives;

NOW people—see the empty lives of the analysts and choose to "get a life." They are not seriously influenced by "traditional people" because they are not psychologically tuned in to their understanding of time as continuous.

These three "generations" span several biological generations. NOW people are likely to be young people. Certainly some younger people are comfortable with continuous time, generally because they grew up in a traditional family with a strong psychological orientation toward continuous time.

One basic foundation for NOW living consists of families who are in their second (or in a few cases, third) biological generation of NOW living. Another origin of NOW living is dissatisfaction with the analytical desert which drives people to escape from time even without prior roots in NOW. They are escaping emptiness. For young people who grew up in NOW families and were not exposed to traditional views, traditional views of continuous time resemble medieval folk tales.

A NOW person is "free at last." There is no tie to a culture inherited from people without names—no tie to marble statues along the Potomac or on the streets of Berlin, Rome, Moscow, London, Delhi, Beijing Tokyo, Madrid—no rope around the free person's waist—no tie to books in libraries.

When we are NOW people in NOW society, we have it all. We are on our own!

And we are tragic, too—tomorrow no one *cares* about today's NOW person—no one appreciates the beauty of her life or his life—there is nothing to leave for others—no reason to leave anything for anyone.

Together, we are a NOW society. Together we do not recognize that there was something else. If life had a past, present, future, there would still be something called "culture." We would listen to its stories. We would like to learn. We are free not to waste time on the "smoke and mirrors" called culture.

Society is a moving river. When the water of a river flows around a rock, it separates into two streams. Past the rock the two streams flow together—they are again a single stream. The rock was "then," but for the river, there's only NOW. Society is only NOW. Culture is like the rock—lost behind us—"upstream somewhere, somewhen."

NOW living does not have norms. It has no culture, no history, no future—just whatever occurs next.

Someone wrote, "God is dead!" What the author *might* have written runs deeper and wider, "No one would *care* if God died." For a society which has escaped from time, "God" is "cultural furniture," from a discarded culture.

God was the centerpiece of American culture. God is still "the centerpiece of the American culture." To our society, It doesn't matter, because the river of American society has flowed past culture. Culture is upstream somewhere. We can no longer see or remember that time or place.

The objective reality of God is not an issue. The issue is society's (society is the composite of all of us) inability to conceive of God because we have escaped from the categories of thinking which offer knowledge of God, or faith in God, or for some people, non-belief, which is called atheism.

There are passages in the Bible which discuss unbelief, but NOW thinking is detached from the language of belief and unbelief. "I don't believe that," simply states dissent from a proposition. If I make that statement, it does not involve me as a person because discussion of these categories is not part of NOW. A statement like "I believe" is a throw-away remark.

Culture is dead! "I don't want any guidelines—only freedom."

NOW

NOW living **is** divorce from culture. Society is swirling downstream from culture.

Can *any* society exist without *some* culture? American NOW society is doing it—going ahead without any guidance. Guidance is impossible because things happen too fast. Institutions can *compel* but cannot *persuade*.

Life is a video game—crashes, death—and suddenly you're alive again, controlling another video vehicle on a different obstacle course, with different enemies.

Life is entertainment. If someone dies, it's a happening. Stop the game, carry her off the field, take him out on the Zamboni, splice in a commercial. The game is good—Interruptions are part of the show.

All the NOW people "got real." They got a life.

There is an occasional hangover. Somebody remembers Uncle Chad. He was an analyst. Uncle Chad said, "There will always be rules. When the last rule is broken and gone, someone will write new rules." We can re-interpret Uncle Chad, "When the old culture is gone, a new one will be born."

What drives NOW?

NOW living is experience—in large print—stimulation and deadening of the central nervous system—uppers, downers, sex, sunshine, spending, exhilaration, all the stuff that someone sells as glamorous.

NOW is "stuff." NOW is faster, bigger, better, daring, hunger for experience, greed for experience, and greed for money. Money is the door-opener to experience—crack or alcohol, sex or speed, power or envy.

NOW is curiosity. IF it's new it's NOW. New drugs for new experiences. New rubs for new bodies. New laws to ramp up new behaviors. Clone a sheep in order to clone pigs in order to clone people in order to be younger longer because younger is faster and NOW is better faster.

NOW is research to stay ahead of anyone else. And maybe the researcher is on the NOW treadmill, even the nerd researcher.

If you think you understand who is a NOW person and if you think nerds cannot be NOW, rethink the thought. Nerds who crack computer security systems are as NOW as country music stars with crowds rioting for tickets to their shows, and they are NOW people in their own special way.

Fame, experience, greed, curiosity, power, control! Gimme it all! More. **Me. NOW.**

Six billion loners on separate NOW trips. Maybe not six billion yet. There are places where NOW society hasn't arrived—remote villages, dictatorships which shut out NOW images. Six billion pieces of society moving outside of time—no past, no today, no future—only instants of NOW, disconnected from other instants of NOW, disconnected from what was and from what will be.

This is what it means to be "free at last."

If six billion people were six billion atoms or 6X billion atoms, activity would just be random until the big cooldown.

But people are not billiard balls bouncing off each other. If people are together, someone tries to build power. Emotions flare. Random behavior gets shaped by others. And structures start to form, and the structures compete with each other, and a framework forms, a framework for shaping all the activity of people—even NOW people. More about that in another chapter.

NOW—apart from time

Clearly, the clock ticks the same for NOW people as for everyone else. Calendar pages turn on the same days for NOW people as for everyone else.

But clocks and calendars are only measuring devices. NOW people have a different *orientation* to time than traditional past-present-future people. NOW people operate by impulse without regard to past or future. Psychologically, they have escaped from the kind of time which is the foundation for Western culture and for cultural institutions.

NOW people live apart from norms and institutions. Rules for NOW people are whatever seems to apply at the current impulse—apart from whatever was once called "normal." "Normal" is "what I want to do right at this moment."

NOW is the only context. In this context, prisons fill, families explode, education is a charade, lives drift.

Society forgets its roots

Society is the composite of the lives of the people. American society can barely remember its historical culture because there is no context for "remembering."

For several decades, the ranks of "traditional" Americans oriented toward chronological time have been getting thinner. These "traditional" people are comfortable with inherited norms and cultural institutions.

If "traditional" Americans think about the NOW society, they might be reminded of Gertrude Stein's remark about a place she didn't like. She wrote, "There is no *there* there." With deep irony, NOW people could equally disdainfully dismiss traditional cultural norms and institutions (AND the analytical lifestyle) by saying the same thing: "There is no *there* there."

This great schism of NON-understanding is a psychological boundary—a barrier between NOW people and people "in tune" with traditional culture. When these two groups of people think about society or think about each other, they think in different categories.

That's where we are today. Two psychological "generations," the "generation" of traditional Americans and the "generation" of NOW people, do not understand one another because they have incongruent time orientations.

A third "generation" (perhaps spanning two biological generations) consists of "analysts" who form a "transition state of society." They are change agents in traditional society and play no role in NOW society.

Change in America

There is a one-way message from NOW people to cultural institutions in America: "We don't want you and we don't need you and we will ignore you." The increasing volume and tempo of the one-way message remind us that NOW oriented people have internalized our social divorce.

The implicit message from NOW people is, "We will get rid of these institutions."

"Traditional" Americans support cultural norms and institutions and try to "control" NOW people. Traditional Americans do not psychologically understand the nature of the social divorce we are living through—even though many perceive that something is radically wrong.

Like traditional Americans, "analysts" do not psychologically comprehend the social divorce taking place, even though the analysts play a role in splitting the society from its cultural moorings—largely because their detached, programmatic behavior inspires others the next generation to "get a life."

As part of "getting a life," the next generation (NOW people) discard what went before. With a broad, sweeping broom they also do away with traditional culture and cultural institutions.

NOW people are cultural orphans—some, by choice, others by accident. They "became orphans" by "rejecting the parent." The NOW generation does not want a cultural parent, but traditional people try to impose the parent on the orphaned NOW generation. Applying old rules cannot work because the NOW generation makes its own rules.

Chapter 6

SOCIETY DIVORCES CULTURE

Society and culture—alive on different levels

Society is a composite of people and how they live. Cultural Institutions and "accepted canons" of behavioral, moral, and ethical norms are "handed down" from earlier generations. Institutions do not define society. The PEOPLE define society through their ways of living.

Baby Boom people matured and the prior generation retired. The activities which define our society changed. NOW society replaced "old-fashioned" society during a transition period of perhaps twenty years. Society moved away from unresponsive cultural institutions and behavioral canons.

The people, especially young people, live by impulse. And the *people are the society*.

For centuries culture grew around philosophers, religious leaders, laws learned from empires and kings and great thinkers. This is our past. The culture is an entity which attempts to govern our present, to shape our actions so the future will look like the past and the present.

But no culture can be as alive as the society it would shape. A culture *lives vicariously* through thought, laws, government, music, business practices and *institutions*. Our culture survives in our institutions. Once a culture is abandoned by its owners, it ceases to change—except through decay.

Society is truly alive. It lives through the actions of its people.

Abandoning the past—divorcing a culture

People who live by impulse have given away the past. It does not interest them. They do not think about future consequences of present actions—not because they don't care, but because future consequences of present actions are not part of their thinking process. Living by impulse—NOW people express who they are.

This living separately from culture is the "social divorce." Impulse people relate *as little as absolutely possible* to the culture. They ignore it because it is not relevant to them.

I recently heard a radio report of a man with 24 drunken driving arrests. Clearly, whatever the culture and its institutions say to him means absolutely nothing. He said goodbye to the culture some time ago. The culture lacks both the will and the popular support to control this person. The institutions will have no effect on the man until the "big hammer" comes down. The "big hammer" will come down on him if he kills someone in an auto "accident." Will that tragedy be an accident or a symptom of a social divorce which no one has acknowledged? One thing is clear: the event is waiting to happen—if not to this man and a random "victim," then to another person and his/her random "victim."

In the meanwhile, many people buy bigger and bigger vehicles to protect themselves from uncontrolled and uncontrollable drivers like that man. In a strange twist of reaction, our crowded roads and the resultant huge thirst for imported oil are part of a much larger pattern of social change.

Impulse disconnects people from reflection, from values, from con-sequences, except as consequences follow from an "unfortunate" clash of an event and an institution which survives as a remnant of the divorced culture.

The culture moves along its own path, and the growing NOW society pays less and less attention to the culture.

Does it really matter if "society" and "culture" drift apart like unmoored ships in the night?

Do the following symptoms of a society at war with its culture and institutions matter?

1. Prisons are overflowing.
2. Welfare costs are being rejected by the formal culture as "too high and growing."
3. Schools are not serving the NOW population. A large segment of NOW people are leaving school because the schools are irrelevant to them. We have chosen the verb carefully, i.e., "schools ARE irrelevant to NOW people," NOT "schools SEEM irrelevant."
4. Skilled jobs (offered by institutions) are increasingly begging for people to fill openings. Technology firms have appealed to the government to increase immigration or "green card" quotas for engineers by 50,000 per year to fill needs which are not being filled by American citizens.
5. Business practices are more frequently cultural residue than relevant to society. This may explain why the most promising avenue for NOW people into the changing economy of a rapidly changing society is through entertainment and the least promising avenue is through a non-relevant educational system. Though relevance does not necessarily create "good" education, non-relevance almost guarantees non-education ("bad" education by almost any definition).
6. *Under*employment (concentrated among NOW people) is growing as the Formal Culture uses automation to replace "being there" jobs with skilled jobs. "Being there" jobs are plentiful in a booming economy, but low unemployment numbers mask high

*under*employment numbers. [Note: a thorough discussion of technology, automation, "full employment," and underemployment would be the subject of a different book.]

7. Pastimes of NOW people are increasingly outside the bounds of "lawful behavior" (as defined by formal culture); these pastimes may include use of unlawful drugs, shoplifting, violent acts.

8. Major "random" crimes are a relatively recent social phenomenon which is spreading. The term "drive by shooting" entered the vocabulary in the 1980s and drive by shootings have spread from the "big city" to "anywhere, USA."

Random acts

Understanding "random" acts and how to reduce them or to learn to tolerate them will come from internalizing what has happened to our people.

Cultural institutions can become equipped to deal effectively with impulse behavior by acknowledging that institutions and cultural norms are not relevant to the behaviors of NOW people, and by recognizing that cultural relevance decreases as the number of NOW people grows.

The formal culture, which was our mother, matured with a sense of continuous time (past, present, future), but NOW people do not think in terms of continuous time. NOW activity does not relate to the formal culture.

NOW people do not perceive time, because their life is a succession of isolated "moments." For NOW people, current action is the only real thing because it what they notice. Current action is, in some ways, *unreal* because it has no context. Life is a series of disconnected events driven by impulse. Events do not connect to each other and do not connect to anything else. Isolated events are noticed because they are "something" instead of nothing.

We sense the irony in a famous quote from Woody Allen, "I like life. It's something to do"—a curious rallying cry for the NOW orientation.

The NOW orientation

"NOW" is disconnected from the "present." "Present" presupposes that there is something else (past and future). NOW presupposes nothing.

The terms "past, present, and future," are in our language, but they are not living descriptions of the world. They are dead historical constructs.

For NOW people only the next action is real. The accepted slogan is "What have you done for me lately?" The newest action follows the newest impulse.

NOW acts are not connected with other aspects of life because each moment is complete in itself. The only context for an action is the impulse which drives the action. It is improper to connect actions with what went before and with what follows. "Life" is a succession of disconnected actions driven by impulses not connected to anything else. In this sense, "NOW" is disconnected from "present."

Free-running impulses

Impulse action is not connected with "present" as understood in the context of past, present, future. Impulse action presents and represents the primal person—apart from culture.

Impulse action represents anticipation acted on apart from reflection or analysis. Impulse action executes a program of anticipation under the influence of emotions.

When an impulse action does not bring unwanted consequences, the tendency for impulsive emotion-driven action may be reinforced.

When impulse action has unwanted consequences, the individual person may judge the action to be "stupid."

Two recently reported crimes tell our story for us.

According to newspaper reports, a man was killed by co-workers because he intended to inform police about some minor crimes in the workplace. Several people (later convicted of murder) killed the man, tied a heavy weight to his body and threw it in a paper-processing vat. The body was soon found, and the murder plot unfolded slowly. Near the paper processing vat was a pulverizing vat; any body thrown in the pulverizing vat would never be found. The body would simply have become part of hundreds of tons of paper-slurry and then processed into some paper product.

The newspaper report quoted someone as saying, "Their only mistake was that they did not throw the body into the other vat (the pulverizing vat)." The person quoted did not suggest that the mistake was in murdering a co-worker. Analysis of how a murder was carried out replaced moral judgment of the act of murder.

In our analytical world, social focus centers on analysis apart from moral judgment about a "crime." In the "old-fashioned" time orientation with a context of past, present, future, social focus saw the roots of a crime in the past and judged the crime in the present—because the crime had "evil/bad" consequences in the future—loss of life for the victim, loss of companionship and income for the victim's family in the future.

The people convicted of roles in the murder acted on impulse—impulse postponed until the "coast was clear." People in their 30s, 40s, 50s lived outside the "old-fashioned," past, present, future orientation toward time. Their oddly amplified response was out of proportion to the victim's decision to inform police of a petty crime.

Newspapers tell another bizarre story about a 16-year old allegedly killed by several other teens for non-payment of $250. Three of the alleged murderers were shot in a car at a park a few weeks later—perhaps multiple suicide, perhaps retaliation, perhaps to cover up a larger circle of lawbreaking. Others were apprehended and later tried on various charges.

How the friends of the three reacted suggests that their friends move between analytical detachment from events on the one hand and a NOW orientation toward time on the other hand.

Two quotes illustrate the mindset of this peer group.

A report on what classmates thought: "The students attitude is that these kids (the accused) were stupid because they didn't plan it better and they got caught. They (fellow students) didn't see anything so awful about the fact that people were dead, but that someone got caught doing it."

Clearly this quote reflects an analytical orientation. Friends of the dead teens occupied themselves analyzing what had happened. The friends did not examine root causes and future consequences of actions—not because they "don't care," but because the categories of past, present, future are not relevant to their lives.

A second quote helps clear up the picture—"Some kids, particularly at this age level, don't really think beyond tomorrow." The police liaison person who said "(they) don't really think beyond tomorrow," used a figure of speech. Even tomorrow is not relevant to people acting on impulse. In their context, "tomorrow" simply means, "When I get out of **here**," (the place where I am now).

In this sense, "tomorrow" means "when I'm in the next block," or "out of this building" or "around the corner" or "when I fade back into the crowd."

Teens who allegedly killed another teen to "discipline" him for not paying $250 were not "analysts." Analysis would have told them two key things:

1. The $250 is gone forever. Corpses don't pay debts.
2. The "price" of future loss of freedom (even if freedom only meant staying a step ahead of formal consequences or ahead of the police)—the price would certainly exceed $250—an amount three teens working together could lawfully earn in a day or two.

Our conclusion? Impulse action—the three alleged killers acted on impulse. They were living in a NOW orientation. What went before, what might come later asked for no thought, no analysis—only action.

"Fairness" redefined

If the larger society judges an impulse action to be "wrong," society may punish the individual and the individual may evaluate society's reaction to be "unfair." Whatever the consequence of an act and of society's response, impulse action is only evaluated after the fact, if at all.

Increasingly, both impulse and later evaluation occur in the context of NOW. The link with "old-fashioned" time is gone.

Social divorce

"Social Divorce" has nothing to do with the splitting of marriages; "social divorce" describes a complex split between Society (the composite activity of people) and Formal Culture (including institutions like government).

Tax laws can "cause" divorce—in the sense of ending a marriage. Two examples:

1. Younger couples cannot afford to pay higher income tax rates for joint returns, so, in some cases, they divorce; for many younger couples, an easier response is just not to marry in the first place.

2. Older couples may find that one partner needs medical assistance and that spending marital resources on that person will impoverish the other person if the sick partner dies; some couples choose to divorce and remain together rather than reduce the survivor to poverty. Some observers call this behavior "greedy." Others say that the couple paid higher taxes for years because they were married, and public policy now demands higher costs from the "well" partner because the couple is married. Critics see this as double injustice.

These two illustrations avoid technical arguments over particular rules. The illustrations suggest that people might normally prefer marriage, but Formal Culture (in this case, government) almost forces people to divorce their spouses. Other aspects of Formal Culture (religious traditions and accepted social customs) promote marriage over co-habitation.

These situations are well-known and widely discussed. They illustrate the divergence between Society (what the people do) and Formal Culture, including its institutions.

This divergence of Society (a reflection of the NOW orientation) from Formal Culture (shaped by continuous time) offers insight into why our formal institutions are unable to build prisons fast enough to house prisoners.

Most people in our prison population operate in NOW time. They are not acculturated to our institutions which demand that "social" behavior be measured by the standards of a different era.

Institutions hold people accountable according to continuous time—past, present, future. "Analysts" operate in a sort of "limbo" between a NOW orientation and the traditional orientation toward time, and they tend to tolerate clashes with formal institutions.

Consider a recent encounter which Nancy (my wife) had with the bureaucracy of the City of Milwaukee. She received a menacing letter, which threatened her credit status and a variety of vague, unspecified consequences if she did not immediately pay a "long-overdue" parking ticket. The license number on the ticket matched hers, but her vehicle had not been in Milwaukee even once during the year in which the ticket was issued. After a phone call, in which she was told she was "lucky" to get through, the city checked with the State of Wisconsin and found that her license plate had never been on the large Ford van which was ticketed. Her little Saturn sedan was "innocent."

The parking ticket was obviously discarded by the driver of the van, but the institution chased the license number until it found Nancy. Then, feeling ignored, the institution wanted retribution. Nancy established her innocence, but we later learned that hundreds of people went through the same problem, and many of them were not "lucky" enough to have their calls answered. Who knows how much trouble they had dealing with a still powerful institution of the dying culture? How much rage results from collisions between institutions and innocent people? How do NOW people react in those situations? How do the "loose cannons" among NOW people react?

There is a profound divergence between institutions and NOW people.

The widening gap between NOW people and Formal Culture is a "Social Divorce." NOW society and formal institutions are separating into two camps. The two camps are almost at war with each other. Quite literally, these two "camps" are becoming "armed camps."

A few of the armed camps operating outside the law are similar to the Branch Davidians of Waco, Texas. Some armed camps are "separate" societies patterned along the lines of continuous time and inherited behavioral norms. These "armed camps are often highly structured and operate far from Formal Culture.

"Armed camps" of NOW people are likely simply to be groups of NOW people who have weapons. "Armed camps" are virtually every-where—in schools, in the workplace, in private homes, and, ultimately, on the street—because they are simply groups of people who make up our society.

Social collapse?

Does it seem possible to you that this social divorce—the unbridge-able gap between how people live and how the culture is built—that this gap could become so wide that social collapse might occur?

If our prisons are too full, our schools lose the fight for excellence, our *under*employed youth are increasingly displaced by automation and lack skills to advance in business (business as cultural institution)—if they become marginalized to the extent of becoming "career" *under*employed (or unemployed)—does it seem that the society will begin to unravel?

Consider how society could unravel.

Consider how the function of society is unravelling:

> School expenditures continue to rise while test scores fall or remain flat. Anecdotal evidence of academic achievement by students suggests that averages do not adequately describe problematic issues in education.

Anecdotes are often chosen for shock value. One compelling story riveted my attention recently. A high school valedictorian in a major metropolitan area was subsequently found to be illiterate. Can anyone learn anything in an environment for which illiteracy marks the *high point* of achievement?

The illiterate valedictorian is not the "fault" of educators or the educational system. It is also not the "fault" of the valedictorian. The "social divorce" gave birth to the embarrassment of the valedictorian and his educators.

The young valedictorian is immersed in the NOW orientation of his society. His educational institution is part of the formal, inherited culture. His educators straddle the growing gap between society and the formal culture. The young man and his "education" were like "ships passing in the night."

Our complex society needs to develop native talents of its valedictorians for society to function effectively.

Thousands of people retire every day. The increasing complexity of society demands that retirees be replaced by people with **greater** skills than they have.

The dependency ratio (the number of people supporting one "dependent"—child, retired, welfare recipient, etc.) was a major focus of discussion when millions of parents were taking care of retirees and raising the children of the baby boom.

Expected dependency ratios dominate discussion of how sound the social security system will be.

Unlawful behavior ("crime"—as our culture defines unlawful behavior), often more impulse-driven than a result of deliberate planning, collides with our institutions with this result: almost two million people are incarcerated.

Several million more people are being "processed" in the "criminal justice system"—some merely "monitored," others under court supervision, others on parole. These millions do not or cannot participate effectively in the labor force. Their families end up on the wrong side of the dependency ratio equation, and all the public employees who "monitor," prosecute, "process," and guard these millions drain productive effort from social system—and the dependency ration worsens still more.

When there were 8-10 workers per "dependent," the dependent burden per worker was significantly lighter than with 3-4 workers per dependent.

An incarcerated person may impose as big a financial burden on society as two or three "ordinary" dependents.

The cost of maintaining formal cultural institutions (schools, health care, prisons, the criminal justice system, eldercare) may grow so large that the society begins to close down large segments of these cultural institutions. The "culture" and our institutions may be our "heritage," but "society" (the aggregate of all people) pays the costs for the institutions.

Cultural institutions are the muscles which carry our inherited cultural norms. As these muscles weaken (because the public cannot afford the cost), the inherited cultural norms fade and society loses its rudder. Society will drift and random, impulse-driven behavior will increase.

Increasing unlawful behavior is a symptom of the social divorce. Breakdowns in education and the dependency burden resulting from unlawful behavior illustrate the effects of the social divorce.

To study what some call the "breakdown of the family" would require a complete book and even then we might have trouble deciding whether the "breakdown of the family was a **result** of the social divorce or a major **cause** of the social divorce.

Or perhaps the breakdown is neither **result** nor **cause**. Perhaps "family breakdown" is part of the whole. Certainly, the NOW orientation cannot readily be linked with the kind of lifelong care that family members lavish on one another in "traditional" societies. Our inherited culture and cultural institutions were shaped by past societies in which family had a broader meaning AND in which family played a greater functional role.

Most of the **productive** aspects that once centered on individual families have moved to industry and the commercial sector of society. We are so far removed from that era that an example is as humorous as illustrative: Shoes were once made by a cobbler and his family. Today most people don't even know that "cobbler" is a word related to shoes. Most people would say a "cobbler" is a kind of dessert.

Grain was once grown on small family farms to feed local people and animals. Corporate farming has largely replaced family farms. Many so-called "family farms" are simply **former** family farms which have grown into corporate farms. Others are hobby farms or land held for investment by former farming families who now support themselves with other types of work.

Clothing was once manufactured in the family from cloth purchased from another family. Clothing production is now a complex maze of international contracts and subcontracts. Almost no one even realizes **where** a particular garment comes from. The label in my newest shirt says "European fabric," but the production label says "Made in Hong Kong." Where is the shirt from? Certainly, most NOW people wearing a one-season (or single-wearing) fashion garment don't even attempt to imagine the face of the person who sewed the garment on another continent so far away that our night is their daytime.

Even many social functions of the family have moved to industry and commerce.

Industry and commerce might find that NOW-oriented people are too "inconvenient" to incorporate into their systems. Corporate enterprises are cultural institutions which serve and sell to society. In this role, corporations **are** a New Business Reality—run by "analysts" to create profit for "owners" of the businesses. Some owners are individuals or a small inside group (close corporation). In some corporations "owners" are shareholders, and often the de-facto "owners" are management—no matter who owns the business "on paper."

Why are NOW people "inconvenient" for business? Increasingly, business expects total commitment of employees. If the 1980s were the decade in which success meant "setting aside family," the 1990s meant "setting aside personal life entirely"—absurd, and "not an option" for NOW people. NOW people in the 21st century are even less likely to accommodate business than NOW people of the 1990s.

For NOW people even the concept of "setting aside personal life" simply does not register. In some sense, the idea is so foreign to their thought structures as to be "nonsense syllables"—an unintelligible foreign language.

Business management **expects** professionals and managers to set aside personal life.

Structural evolution of business is rapidly excluding the middle. At the top are managers and high-powered analysts who set aside personal life. The old industrial and commercial "middle" is being replaced by computerized systems. In the former paradigm, the middle consisted of many important bureaucratic functions overlaid with "experienced" managers. These functions are being automated or contracted out to specialty firms which automate similar processes for a broad range of client firms.

A third broad category of industrial/commercial work is production and service work. "Workers"—increasingly drawn from NOW-oriented people are viewed by managements as "costs" to be phased out when possible:

1. Sales people to be replaced by standardizing sales approaches and selling through computerized 800-number systems (systems which will later be replaced by automated Internet services)
2. Production workers to be replaced by automated machinery

Opportunities remain at the interface between highly automated commercial ventures and the general public. These interface positions are filled by people whose primary function is to make clients feel at ease and comfortable enough to purchase goods/services from the enterprise. The actual "sales" situation is between a system and a client, even when the apparent "sales" situation is between the interface person and the client. These interface people are clearly vulnerable to further advances in automation.

However measured, millions of positions filled by NOW-oriented people early in the 21st century will be eliminated through automation and **under**employment will increase. America already has a supply of Ph.D. taxi drivers and discount store checkout clerks.

As underemployment grows, NOW people have decreasing motivation to pursue a cultural institution which wants them "for fill-ins" until they can be phased out. NOW people consciously avoid the New Business Reality because of its demands to choose between work and personal life.

Whether by prior choice or by business decisions beyond their control, the NOW orientation is validated by experience—"If business doesn't **really** want me, why shouldn't I live for NOW?"

The social divorce may accelerate if these developments follow the scenario sketched above.

NOW-oriented people with decreased opportunities to work **within** the cultural institutions have no compelling reason to support the formal culture. If social stresses grow, society may force changes in structural cultural institutions through politics or through the growth of a shadow-culture operating alongside the formal culture and institutions.

What is a "shadow culture?" A shadow culture begins with a fringe group. Most of these fringe groups have a short life span, but through a process of weeding out, some survive, and eventually one or two shadow cultures compete to become dominant. The growth of Christianity in the Roman Empire is a notable example of a transition from shadow culture to the official religion of an empire. Whatever we think of that transition, many transitions from shadow culture to dominant culture are extremely unhappy.

In Germany, after World War I, two cultures fought openly in the streets while the "dominant" culture slumbered on in Berlin and Weimar and other places. The shadow cultures were the Nazi movement and the Communist movement. We know the rest of that history.

In Russia during World War I Bolshevism competed with liberal Socialism. We know the rest of that history.

In America, shadow cultures alive and dead include:
1. The Ku Klux Klan
2. MOVE—an urban black separatist group
3. The Branch Davidians in Waco, Texas
4. Many "militias"—mostly white, mostly rural
5. A gray market economy which is not formally organized but operates with informal guidelines to help people avoid state and federal taxes. Without the "lost" taxes avoided through the gray market many aspects of the formal culture are starved for funds, especially the public sector of our formal institutions. As this occurs, institutions become weaker and are subject to institutionalized corruption instead of occasional "shocking" instances of abuse which are endemic in all bureaucracies.

In summary, a complete social divorce will bring social and cultural changes which over time will be unmanageable.

Are there **positive** aspects to the social divorce? Yes, in spite of what seems negative in the discussion above, the social divorce has many positive qualities. Socially stultifying aspects of the culture are discarded—"whites only" was one of the early discards in a long series of changes.

Dying culture

No culture survives long without an active society which accommodates itself to the culture as a necessary partner. If a culture is discarded, it dies. Remnants may be "rescued" and incorporated into a new culture when a new culture takes shape. In the meanwhile, society drifts toward instability.

Our NOW society has divorced its former culture and that culture is dying. Because the institutions of the culture are powerful and still have powerful backing, the institutions are merely moribund and not yet on their deathbeds, but the culture is dying—because it is being abandoned by larger numbers of people every day and because the supporters of the divorced culture are primarily older people whose lives are nearly over.

NOW Society has already moved on beyond the point where it would even consider re-instituting the culture of continuous time. An era is past.

We escaped the culture of continuous time when—as a Society—we escaped from time.

PART THREE

OPEN-ENDEDNESS

Chapter 7

Freedom!

We have cut ourselves adrift from our inherited culture. We are free!

We are free at last. There are no bounds—no bounds for behavior; no chains of morality; we still have laws, but they are fading away—fading away because we hate them and ignore them: science postpones death; genetics and cloning hint that death might disappear—the last barrier is crumbling.

We are free to do what we want to do now. All that matters is—don't put off what you want to do! Do it

NOW!

Society

What is society? Society is all of us and what all of us do—sometimes one by one, sometimes in groups, sometimes all together. All of us and all of our activity—this is what society is. Society is action! That's us in the third millennium—a volcano of bubbling energy ready to run over the rim of the crater and spill out on everything around. Nothing like our society has ever been before. We are the first generation without the chains of culture. We have tossed the old, outdated culture out the window. We soar like an immortal bird.

Culture

What is culture? Culture is a set of rules and habits, customs and institutions that have guided every society before our society. All those other societies had inherited laws, music, traditions, religions, ways of life passed from one generation to another. All other societies had chains from the past. They were prisoners of someone else's way of life. Those societies lived to pass something on to another generation—to pass on a burden for another generation to carry—worse than ancestor worship—the burden grew—waiting for someone to stop passing it on—waiting for someone to be free. That someone is all of us. We are the first people ever to be free.

If any reader thinks the divorce from culture is simply one author's pipe dream, consider these holidays: Memorial Day marks the beginning of summer travel; the Fourth of July brings fireworks. Do these holidays have any other meaning in the public psyche? It's doubtful. Thanksgiving has lost all its religious significance. Christmas Eve, often described as the "holiest night of the year," is a last bastion for defenders of the now divorced culture; Christmas Day is included in that last bastion, but only until noon.

Few Christians, even those who are part of traditional society—those for whom time is continuous—dare to defend the centrality of Good Friday to American culture. The societal divorce reduced a focal point of the Christian heritage, Good Friday, to an inconvenience. Good Friday as a special day in the Christian memory has no special significance to American society. And what about Easter, the crowning celebration of Christianity? A prominent display in a discount store pictured a smiling little girl holding a tiny chick and said "*Easter, trés chick.*" Easter, has become an excuse for a cute joke for marketers. The once dominant faith is mocked, not merely overlooked. Traces of Christianity as a focus of American consciousness through its cultural memory are irrelevant because cultural memory itself is irrelevant.

For us there is no history, no god, no tradition, no set of rules to follow, no law worth our attention.

The story we are reading is the story of how this happened, how we became free—and—the story of what might happen if "NOW" becomes "THEN."

The rest of the story is called "Toward another culture." You could skip ahead to that rest of the story, but the end of this story is the beginning of another story, so stay with this story to see it unfold.

What next?

Society outran culture in America. The old culture is gone. There is no new culture to replace it.

A new "Wild West" is being born. When the first "Wild West" was born, cultural rules from Europe and New England were left behind. The new "Wild West" is all of us—a new society.

The West grew a new society—and *then* a new "culture." What was left of "Europe" dried up.

America, during the "zeroes" ('00, '01…'09) and "teens" of our new century is beginning without cultural rules, nothing from the past to hold us back. Whoever tries to "preserve our heritage" will be ignored or laughed off the stage. No one person will "shape the new America." America will re-shape itself.

Can we make an educated guess about what will happen? Yes! Is our guess a prediction? Only sort of. When a snowstorm comes, forecasters generally know a storm is coming. Then, they guess where the deepest snow will fall and how much. In 1999 we were housesitting in Coon Rapids, Minnesota. A storm was beginning. Educated "weather guessers" talked about 6-8 inches of snow, with spots of ten inches. We had sixteen inches and shoveled for several days, unwilling to use a formidable high-tech snowblower.

The "zeroes" and the "teens" of the 21st century look like a coming storm. We make educated guesses but are short on facts.

Telecom, genetically altered food, genetically altered people, more global warming, second and third generation Internet, a hundred million people worldwide with HIV, smarter smart cards, less paper money, "who gets the water?," more rebels, new religions, Gen X muscles out the Boomers, gen Y celebrates, Gen Z gets religion,—

Will anyone recognize America? New politics, new heroes, gambling for escape, boredom.—

Scattershot culture

America operates without a generally accepted culture. Laws are tolerated, but flouted when possible. Culture, posing as social norms, is largely overlooked.

Informal rules surrounded by a larger framework of literature, poetry, classical music, plays, and social customs once formed a "culture"

Society paid attention to that culture—two kinds of attention:

1. *Almost always* at least lip service, and
2. *Usually* some actual shaping of behavior to fit the accepted culture.

Millions of schoolchildren heard a story about how Abraham Lincoln walked several miles when he was young—to return a penny which belonged to someone else. The story was told in classrooms all across America (at least in the North) to inspire honesty. To some extent that kind of cultural "story" did work.

There is no longer any accepted culture to guide society. Society is simply a large collection of individuals "doing their own thing" or "doing what their peers do."

Does this mean nobody follows any culture? Hardly. We have adopted a "scattershot culture."

Group cultures are not new. There was an "Old South" and then a "New South." There was "Puritan Boston," then an "Irish Boston," then an "Italian Boston." There was a "German Milwaukee," a "German Chicago," a "Polish Chicago," a "Black Chicago."

Each local culture lived under one or several "umbrella cultures"— the "Old Country," "Americanism," people's church identity, and other subgroup identities.

These "old" groups had strong local flavors. "Boston Irish" thought of themselves as better than "New York Irish," at least in Boston, but different thoughts prevailed in New York.

A broad collection of "should" and "ought" rules steered what people and groups did, but most of those "shoulds and oughts" had a common background in Christian Europe.

Those "old cultures" are gone. There might be lip service to some aspects of those old cultures. "Norwegians" from the Midwest, "Jews" from New York or Chicago. "Blacks" from Detroit or LA People may claim a label without even a foggy notion of what the label means. When the King of Norway visited a "Norwegian" festival in the Midwest he was astonished to see people doing things long forgotten in Norway. Of all the "Norwegians" in the Midwest hardly one in a hundred can say something significant in Norwegian in a way that would be recognized in Norway.

American Scattershot Culture justifies what people actually do. We parody Mao Zedong when we "let a thousand kinds of behavior bloom." Not far behind the thousand behaviors "a thousand cultures are flowering."

Behavioral Inflation

A long-time resident of Lake Tahoe in California had to move out because he could no longer afford to live there. He complained, "The billionaires are driving out the millionaires." That's inflation of money and property values.

The old American culture with its neat subcultures died along with the birth of "NOW." "A thousand behaviors blooming" is a figure of speech for *behavioral inflation*. We could just as well say "a million behaviors blooming."

"Groups" come together in cyberspace. A group might be an assortment of people who never met. In the Internet a "12-year old girl" might be a 58-year old man; a "banker" might be a mortician; a "headhunter for a Fortune 500 firm" might be an unemployed cook sitting in a cybercafe. Virtual people form virtual groups.

For some people a virtual life might be adequate. "Virtual" lives and virtual groups will gradually develop rules for virtual cultures.

Place is not important for NOW people. Their society is where the action is—action they create.

College and high school students go to warm places in March, but place is not a reason. They go because it's warm and clothes are optional. They go for an extended NOW experience. No one stays too long because that kind of NOW takes money and money has become "real" where past and future are only directions on a clock or pages on a calendar.

People who leave jobs angry or who are angry in school do "whatever it takes." They act out their nightmares and their hates. It's easy to do in NOW society because cultural shackles are gone.

Angry people might build a small unit of culture—another chunk of "scattershot culture" to justify what they intend to do anyway. The units of "culture" which remain are units of flexible culture, units to be stretched or compressed to fit the instant—the impulse. Society lurches into the future without a discernible culture which relates to an identifiable whole. There is no identifiable whole.

Chapter 8

Troubles

Social stress

NOW behavior both changes society and has been influenced by society.

Society faces greater and accelerating change caused by NOW behavior. Society had a long history of adapting to a dominant culture which restrained the pace of social change. In the 21st century, the situation is reversed. Society dominates culture and forces rapid change in the culture.

Exceptions to the dominance of culture over society occurred occasionally when a society was conquered by an outside group with a different culture: Turks overwhelmed Constantinople and imposed a new culture; Rome occupied Gaul and Britain and brought Roman culture; Europeans became the dominant population in North America and Native American cultures were forever changed.

Occasionally a culture changes through internal pressure. Science changed culture through learning and technological innovations. The pressures of science changed many aspects of culture. It was hardly necessary to have laws governing speed when horse-drawn wagons were the fastest vehicles in use. With high-speed motor vehicles, institutions added laws to control speed.

The escape from time is not a technological innovation. It is a social innovation. We are creating an internal separation of society from culture which is without precedent. We do not have a prior model to show us what to expect.

Possible outcomes

Consider a series of possible outcomes—with positive and negative connotations.

Various outcomes are not mutually exclusive. There can be more than one outcome, and one outcome does not imply another. They occur as independent events.

1. Society completes a divorce from Christianity. Clearly, North American society once thought of itself as "Christian." Though possibly still Christian in name, North American society is anything *but* Christian.
2. Society consumes and borrows, with little saving or thought for the longer term. Personal obligations and debts threaten instability when the economy weakens.
3. Random (unpredictable and disconnected) behavior escalates—drugs, casual or random sexual encounters, children to whom no one has a commitment, street violence, acts of rage.
4. Cults without commitment, i.e., cults of NOW, without commitment. These cults are generally NOT followed on the basis of commitment—unlike current cults which often demand complete, long-term allegiance.
5. Radical political parties—left, right, eclectic; single-interest, perhaps even single-issue parties.
6. A rise in begging, petty thievery, gypsy-style living.
7. An increase in "discarded children."
8. Re-emerging retreats (monasteries, etc.).

9. Private corporations with paramilitary aspects and long "enlistments."
10. Loss of social organization
11. Widening gulf between the few and the many (an increasing percentage of the many and a decreasing percentage of the few, particularly in education and wealth)
12. NOW behavior can be introduced through disturbances in existing patterns of life. The fire at the Chernobyl reactor in the Ukraine resulted in an enormous release of radioactive material, which—because of wind patterns—affected Belarus (formerly the Byelorussian Republic of the Soviet Union) more than any other area. Governmental and quasi-governmental institutions in Belarus have instituted programs to motivate radiation victims to participate in society. These victims tend to exhibit NOW behavior in an extreme focus on the immediate, with no feeling of participation in any future. For many of them, the past is represented by the nightmare of the fallout, and their expectations of a short life erase all vestiges of hope for a future.

These phenomena in Belarus are loosely parallel to the decades-long pattern of welfare dependence for many NOW people in America. Their past is represented by an unprecedented relationship to a system which reduced the rewards of personal initiative by withdrawing systemic rewards (welfare checks) in rough parallel with individual effort.

In Belarus, nothing an individual can do will alter the fact of exposure to crippling, life-shortening radiation. In the case of welfare, there seems to be nothing an individual can do to release that person from dependence. Clearly, there is a distinction between these two examples. In Belarus the facts are sealed in each individual's damaged genetic and community and psychological structure. The "facts" of welfare are inscribed in the psychological structure of the individual and the community but not in the genetics of the persons involved. It seems that the similarities between these two groups outweigh the differences.

13. For many, there is an *expectation* that things will not work. This is particularly true in some countries of the former East Bloc where individuals have come to regard economic dysfunction as normal. For these people, effort is not rewarded because the existing system is incapable of rewarding effort, except in marginal cases—at the highest and the lowest levels. Inflation frequently nullifies the efforts of people at the lowest levels, leaving them to enjoy what they can in the NOW.

In America, the expectation of many NOW people is shaped by disinterest in a past which has left them without a path to participation in the mainstream and without a psychological link to the future. Thus, their behavior is equally NOW-oriented.

Good and bad in NOW society

Good is "fast with what I want," bad is "slow with what I want." Good" is when major players like government, corporations, scientists are working to solve "my" problem (AIDS, diabetes, crime). "Bad" is when my piece of pie is shrinking or maybe not growing as fast as the next person's slice of pie (too small a military budget, if I work in the defense industry; too big a military budget if I'm a pacifist or if some of the military procurement funds could have been used on "my" project).

"Good" and "bad" are contextual for a NOW person. The context is NOW. A society's activities create and shape that society's culture. Perhaps culture once shaped society. How outdated! How sentimental! How sad the whole idea seems—like total loss of freedom—chained to irrelevance.

Entertainment's the thing! Surf your TV on a fall Saturday. Watch two football teams you've never heard of, from a state you've never been to. Listen to the buildup for players who will vanish into thin air, never to be heard from again. NOW people watch because they're bored. The game is the only thing happening at that moment, and NOW can never be empty. The scenario is repeated in winter, when basketball teams pass across the screens of America like meteors—"awesome" one day and never heard of again.

Greed

With all the goodies that NOW offers, there's rarely too much money. If a person cannot possibly consume all the earnings or assets he/she has, there's the prestige and power of still more assets. NOW society has a pecking order—partly money, partly being seen in the "right" place with the "right" people. With enough money, a person can be with almost anyone in almost any place. The vast majority of NOW people are not wealthy and can't be seen in famous NOW places, so they buy into NOW activities, consume NOW things, wear NOW clothes.

Consuming at NOW levels means running harder to stay in place. NOW people will not give up their leisure (they remember the cry, "Get a life!"), but they don't join (old-line clubs and organizations are dead). NOW people have checked out of their churches, and have almost checked out of their families. Family life has vanished for millions. NOW living is:

+ Doing things, and
+ Having money (or looking like you have money).

Every NOW day is a race from "getting" to "doing." Joining organizations, doing religious things, doing family things—all pushed aside. Organizations, religion, families are leftovers from a time-oriented world. Most organizations represent a sentimental past or an unreal future. Family is easy to neglect because they are always "available." Children raise themselves or are coached by peers.

If you (reader) are put off by these descriptions of NOW living, either you think we are lying or you don't like the picture. What we are writing is like a weather report. When the weather is described on TV, the meteorologist might say, "It rained an inch overnight." One listener says, "Great, my lawn needs it." Another says, "My expensive new grass seed was washed away. I'll have to pay to seed the lawn all over again." Our report on NOW society is like a weather report. We report what we see happening.

Curiosity

In an old Greek legend, Pandora was ordered not to open a magic box. Her curiosity grew and she did open the box. Out flew all sorts of wonders and tricks, misfortunes and bad luck. Curiosity has its own price.

Scientists are curious, so they perform brand new experiments every day. Remember how boring physics class was? Did you roll a ball down an inclined plane and time it to see how long it took, measure its final speed and see if the law of gravity worked in your high school? It was boring because someone else did it before you were born and because the class ahead of you did it and because the physics teacher had the worst monotone voice you ever heard.

Real scientists do new things, NOW things. For NOW scientists there are no consequences from their experiments, only excitement or momentary fame—maybe a patent, maybe money, probably a mention in the local press, and—always possible—a Nobel Prize. If something bad happens, perhaps an entire species disappears, it simply happens. The scientist doesn't own the problem; everyone does. The scientist shares this new problem with 6 (going on 7) billion other people.

You may have your own science horror story—how curiosity got out of hand. The legend of Pandora is our warning. In some ways, the Greeks were NOW people. They did what was new. They lived a sort of NOW life. Like us, some of them lived apart from time and lived apart from consequences. For them, FATE was going to have its way in any case.

Examine the NOW face of science and discovery. People climb Everest because they can afford to do it, because they can claim fame and because they're curious.

A theory of unpredictable change

Bizarre things become common because NOW emerges from a "push" milieu. A commercial slogan written on the computer mouse pad I use says, "It's not about reaching limits. It's about rising above them." The mathematician in me is horrified by that slogan. The NOW person in me says, "So what's new about that?"

One recently emerging branch of thought is called (by an unfortunate name) "catastrophe theory" (CT). CT says that when certain limits are broken, totally different behavioral characteristics take over. After a (technically named) "catastrophe," old laws just don't apply. New laws have taken over. It's almost as though a helicopter picked up a hockey team and dropped it in the middle of a soccer game. Everything is different. The best hockey skates are useless in the new context.

CT describes radical and abrupt change—change outside known bounds, change beyond normal expectations of someone living on the "before" side of that change. In a technical sense, radical changes often fit the definition of a "catastrophe," but many of those "catastrophes" are beneficial or "good" changes. The birth of a child is one of those "good" changes.

Before birth, the fetus receives oxygen via the mother's blood and the placenta. "Air" as we know it is not part of its experience. Birth, in this sense, is a "catastrophe" (we reiterate: the original theorists might have chosen a less jarring name for their new "catastrophe" theory) because the world of the fetus is completely changed—in just a minute or a few at most. The "old" is gone forever and the new is totally different, some would say "violently different." Catastrophe Theory outlines how such radical shifts can happen. Former "rules" are replaced with strangely different "rules." The "former" is strange and alien and usually can't be brought back. Nothing "works" the same.

Another example: Russia's shift from a centrally-planned economy to a market economy. Don't even think about "better" or "worse." Events of the 1990s and of the new century in Russia illustrate that a society which operates under one economic paradigm might not be prepared for a new paradigm. There is no parallel for the changes in the economy of the former Soviet Union. No one had ever experienced life in a market economy. Patterns learned in the centrally planned economy didn't work and new patterns were not given enough time to work as changes piled up too rapidly.

Consider this example from my first visit to the Soviet Union. In the city of Tallinn (Estonia), I noticed unusual color schemes on a neighborhood of apartment buildings. My own experience was from a market economy. I asked our tour guide, "Do the colors (muted pink and yellow) on these buildings reflect a regional tradition?" The woman leading the tour answered, "No, these were the colors available when this neighborhood was re-painted." My paradigm (mental rule) was "choice." Her paradigm (and the Soviet paradigm) was "availability."

Another example of a social shift—mind control of a person entering a "cult." One technique used by many cults is very simple: when a person shows some interest in the cult, the person is surrounded by new friends. It's subtle, not overt. The new recruit has lots of new friends—not suddenly, but in a closed sequence of activities, one right after another. If the recruit tries to withdraw, cult members act "hurt." Soon the recruit is exhausted and is becoming "programmed"—indoctrinated so that what the cult wants and does feels "right" and other activity is uncomfortable, especially activities which pull the initiate away from the cult—activities with the recruit's family or previous friends. The quicker family and friends are out of the picture, the quicker and surer a total change to the new social setting. When the recruit is indoctrinated, he/she is not able to choose to leave the cult.

"Going back" without outside help is psychologically impossible. The recruit's social paradigm is totally changed. Catastrophe Theory (CT) explains this shift—one set of "rules" is replaced by a new set of "rules." The "game" has changed.

Confusion

Scientists, noting a 99% overlap in genetic coding among chimpanzees and people, join in a chorus of attack on religious views.

Jim, age 33, observed "How can scientists be so certain of their 'primal soup' hypothesis? Is the idea of God any more preposterous than the collision of atoms in a void leading to the Internet Age?"

A small city in Missouri has a four-quadrant city logo. One quadrant of the logo has two curved lines which look vaguely like the shape of a fish. A group of people from outside the city attacks the logo in court under the banner of "civil liberty"—attacks because a fish symbol is used by some Christians as one symbol among many. Should all road intersections be at strange angles so they won't look like crosses on maps?

Secular society on the offense—religion on the defense— along with philosophy and law

Does the secular attack matter?

Perhaps not. This book is about people gathered together in a big conglomerate called "society"—and about this society's divorce from its "culture."

Each society is partially guided by its own "North Star"—a blend of philosophy, laws, art, religion, music and traditions often called "culture." What happened to the American "North Star" of social behavior? Do individuals follow this "star?" Does the larger group ("society") follow this "star?"

Let's look at the pieces of "culture" and then decide what influence culture has.

1. Religion on the defensive. People feel forced to "apologize" for being religious—especially for being Christian, because Christianity is closely identified with the birth of institutions rooted in Continuous Time.
2. Philosophical fashion changes so fast and so often that it "comes full circle" in a generation and then begins to circle again. Only professional philosophers know what other philosophers are saying, and they are unable to tell the rest of us what all the jargon means.
3. How about the law? Is law dependable as a social guide?

Recently, we sold a house. Our real estate attorney is very meticulous. He drafted a long sales contract according to current standards, and he complained about the ever-growing wall of paperwork. No one and no one company wants to handle an entire transaction, so expanding masses of middlemen and middle-organizations handle bits and pieces of a real-estate transaction. Costs of transactions rise without any seeming cap. Our attorney offered these words of cheer, "New laws and rules are on the books every day. Even the law reviews have trouble keeping up."

This very gifted attorney works exclusively with real estate and often does the paperwork for multi-million dollar commercial transactions. His off-the-record comments make me think that the old saying "Buyer beware!" has gone through two changes—first to "Seller beware!" and then to "Everyone beware!"

Law as a labyrinth

Often law is a drag on society. At worst, law is useless. It even contributes to social decay by undermining common sense approaches to keeping society workable. A newspaper report early in the new century cited an incident involving the seizure of 200 pounds of cocaine. The "street value" of the cocaine was over a million dollars. The case died in court because the defendants were not informed that the FBI had assisted local police. People dealing in millions of dollars of illegal substances are professionals who know that their capabilities and contacts place them beyond the reach of local police. They also know how to avoid prosecution in most instances. Even a casual observer can understand this, but our outdated legal system often applies more stringent criteria to parking violators than to professional drug dealers.

Look at what's happened to the law and health care. In June 1998, the U.S. Supreme Court added HIV infection to the list of disabilities which qualify for government funding and other assistance. During the same month a close friend was turned down by Medicare for a PSA test (a test which helps measure whether a person has prostate cancer and how serious an existing prostate cancer is). This man has already been diagnosed with prostate cancer. The PSA test helps determine when serious surgery and radiation are needed.

What does this contrast between the Supreme Court ruling and the Medicare ruling prove? Nothing! The contrast proves nothing because you already know that the law is no longer dependable in offering real guidance for society. In the medical field law is useless! Period!

What about criminal law? Two stories from Wisconsin reported by the Associated Press in an issue of our local newspaper in June, 1998 illustrate that law can harm more than it helps.

Case 1. A twelve year old male forcibly raped a thirteen year old girl on several occasions. She subsequently gave birth to a baby boy, which she disposed of in a plastic bag. The infant died. The twelve year old alleged rapist is by law (his age) not punishable, but the girl (a few months older) faces murder charges. In this case the law makes the victim of forcible rape guilty and the criminal is protected by law. We can assume that she, under the stress of an unchosen pregnancy, was less able to deal with her dilemma in an adult fashion than the male, whose superior strength wiped out her rights as well as her mental health.

Case 2. A six year old boy picked up a few wet firecrackers from a lawn on the way to school. The boy is in legal trouble—thrown out of school for bringing "pyrotechnic devices" to school. Does anyone believe the six year old ever heard of "pyrotechnic devices?" Would YOU be alarmed about a small, soggy firecracker?

Most Americans are aware that our prisons are filling and our laws are emptying. Laws incapable of distinguishing forcible rape ("innocent" offender) from kindergarten curiosity ("guilty" curious pre-literate child) have ceased serving as a "guiding star" for society.

Public behavior is no longer steered by philosophy, by religion, by law. It is the product of impulse.

Tradition and other aspects of culture

Ask any NOW person you meet, "Does tradition influence you?" One of two answers is likely:

1. "Gimme a break! Get real!"
2. "What's tradition?"

Art—another of our laundry-list of norms which once helped to guide behavior—

Art *does* influence behavior—with a difference. NOW art reflects NOW society. NOW art brings nothing new to the table—brings nothing of what *was* culture. NOW art is a mirror showing NOW people how they are behaving—NOW people like what they see in NOW art. NOW art *affirms* NOW behavior, *amplifies* NOW behavior. Any other art is part of tradition and is ignored.

NOW behavior ignores inherited culture. There is almost no connection between NOW behavior and culture which would bring the past into the present as a guide to the future.

Philosophy—   vague and useless.

Religion—   discarded.

Law —   complicated, confused, comical, pathetic

Tradition— something which happened at least once before—except when a group stages an event and announces, "We are starting a tradition."

Art— NOW art makes NOW people feel good; ignore the rest.

Chapter 9

Immigrants to Life

NOW is our new country. We are immigrants in the land of NOW.

Unless you are a Native American, you came from somewhere else or your "grandparents" came from somewhere else. You are an immigrant or your "great…great…great, etc" were immigrants. Some other society and some other culture are "back there somewhere," but it doesn't matter. You are here, not there.

When new Americans were immigrants, they built a new society and a changing culture. They totally ignored Native American culture. The Native American culture was *someone else's* culture.

This time around people in America have outgrown what was *their own* culture—outgrown philosophy, religion, law, tradition and outgrown art with any content beyond a self portrait.

What next?

Strange dawn

America is not the only society changing too fast for its former culture to keep up.

Increasingly, people around the world are immigrants in their own countries. Rapid changes stemming from politics, restructured economies, mobility, and technology trigger rapid changes in how people act.

Patterns of daily life shift so rapidly in some societies that entire populations act like immigrants. Restructured societies disconnect from their inherited cultures. People in these newly forming societies act in an exploding wave of NOW behaviors—partly because of pressures from the disappearance of old institutions and partly due to the tidal wave of influence from the American media.

Recently I was in Sinaia, Romania. After a three day meeting, the group visited the Transylvanian village of Bran, where Bran Castle of the legendary Count Dracula guards the former frontier with Wallachia. The castle, high on a steep outcropping and full of narrow stairways and secret passageways, was built as a fortification to enforce tax collections on merchant trade passing through.

The small village of Bran has few tourists and most of the visitors are either Romanians or from cities in Northern Europe. Even so, the tour guide spoke to the group in American-style English. No one in the group was from England and I was the only American, but the influence of America and its language is hard to escape—even in remote villages. Dreams of legendary wealth are sold by the media as a reality in the American way of life, and people everywhere are following the dream. Their societies may soon change even faster than American society, and their cultures will certainly not keep up.

When we left Sinaia on the next day, our driver and the Romanian woman who organized our meeting took us to Bucharest to catch our planes back to our different ways of life—one man to France, one to Germany, two to Austria, one to Poland, and me off to Switzerland before returning to Wisconsin. On the ride to Bucharest, the radio blasted out American music as we wound down the curvy roads of the Southern Carpathian foothills and past oil fields bombed by American planes during World War Two. Romanians are running hard to remake their society according to a pattern they have seen only on TV or in films—an American pattern, unbelievably foreign to their former way of life, whether communist or pre-communist.

One colleague at the meeting in Romania was from Kiev in the Ukraine. I asked him to send me a story of change from his own society. How do people act? What is society like in the former USSR?

Here's the example he e-mailed to me after he returned to Kiev: "In the former USSR, when people on the train began to eat their lunch they would offer to share their food with other people in the compartment.

"Now most people no longer do that. Only people from villages still follow the old ways.

"In the former USSR, people felt themselves to be part of a unified whole—Soviet People. Now, life is more individualistic. Historically (even before Soviet times) the people—especially in villages, felt a common bond. Life on collective farms reinforced the old ways, but now that way of living is disappearing. It is replaced by individualism."

Another friend—this one from Moscow—wrote somewhat differently, suggesting that separation of people by individualism does devalue people, *but* that the Soviet state had already devalued people. This man had taken substantial risks, especially to his career as a research mathematician, by becoming a Christian before the Soviet Union collapsed.

He wrote, "Soviet rule (with its many positive features!) created many negative rules of behavior. The state, run by the 'dictatura' [party officials who held high-level and mid-level offices], did not respect the individual person.

"There are many examples:

1. As a rule, cars do not stop when pedestrians go. Drivers (they are also pedestrians) do not respect someone who has no car. There are many accidents and many victims." [Author's note: I experienced this during my stay in Moscow when the Communist Party was still in charge. A companion and I were crossing a road leading out of the Kremlin when a large black car sped out

of the gate with no regard for us. Clearly, if we had not dodged—
and quickly—we might have been killed. The car of that high-
ranking official would not have stopped if we had been killed.]

2. "Stores generally keep one half of a two-part door closed, mak-
    ing it difficult for customers but easier for the administration."
    [Author's note: This is one tiny example of why market reforms
    are doing poorly in Russia.]

Depersonalization and rapid change make many people immigrants
in their own countries.

Change in Africa has been at least as fast-paced as in former East Bloc
countries. Millions of Africans who grew up in isolated rural villages are
moving to huge cities where they are quickly lost in faceless crowds.
They leave companionship and friends who could help them with
problems and often they can't cope with what they find in the city.

A colleague who helps ship donated medical supplies to a country in
the Southern part of Africa told me that between 28% and 32% of the
entire population of Zimbabwe already suffers from HIV infection and
the percentage is growing constantly. Rapid migration of people to
cities and movements of large numbers of trucks, coupled with low
incomes for many women has generated unprecedented social change.
Old sexual taboos evaporated and the support of community, family,
and friends was replaced by the need for cash each day. Some nations in
Southern and Eastern Africa have not yet developed a national culture
and the fragmented culture they do have is not adequate to help them
deal with their existing situation.

Many in Africa are penniless beggars in their own home towns. Many
more are beggars or criminals in large, ungovernable cities. In this situation new cultures are being born—most of them ad hoc and some of
them very strange.

Social collapse? Why not?

When a power grid fails, electricity goes down in several states, and the power is out for a day. When the lights go out and the sun goes down, looting begins. What is the looting if not a short-term social collapse? And when did Americans start thinking that looting their neighbors' homes or business places is a good idea whenever looting is possible with low risk of being caught?

Society is mutating—away from its roots—in the direction of "More! Me! Now!"

A friend worked 16 years for a local company. Another company in the same business bought her company. She had earned her way out of weekend work and had earned the right to a reasonable sick-leave bene-fit—which she never used, but might need some day. The new company offered her a big cut in pay, chopped off her sick leave, and said, "Now you can work weekends again." The new owners trashed the past, trashed her loyalty, for bigger profits and stock option benefits for the managers who hacked up my friend's career. Do you know anyone who felt the same axe? A steady stream of personnel moves and corporate restructuring along with frequent sales of various business units became a standard business practice in the 1980s and was raised to a science in the 1990s. In the 21st century the ever more fluid relationship between employer and employee is another aspect of NOW society.

Road rage. A few months ago the first study was published on "road rage." Road rage is new and it's all the rage—another social mutation of the 1990s continuing to escalate in a new century.

Automatic weapons were stockpiled by free-wheeling militias thought to be kooks living "out there" somewhere. As social mutation accelerated, what used to be "ordinary bank robberies" became slaugh-ters. Next, the army gave some police forces automatic weapons. The level of violence in what was "ordinary street crime" escalated and another mutation happened. Crime became armed skirmishes—urban warfare. Underequipped police called for military weapons to hold their own against the militias.

"Hello, Bosnia West?"

What would make anyone think that the mutation toward armed conflict in the cities is over? Is it more likely just beginning?

No one is likely to solve the mystery surrounding the crash of TWA Flight 800, but a lingering question remains—could it really have been a shoulder-mounted missile launched from a Long Island beach?

If the answer is "Yes," then a few people really do know that spreading conflict has begun—and that social mutation is more advanced than most people realize.

If the answer is "No," then hundreds of thousands of people will always wonder—especially anyone who knew anyone on that plane—and maybe thousands more who fly along the South Shore beaches of Long Island. The fact that we wonder is another step in our social mutation—away from our roots in an orderly society with customs and traditions and laws—and toward an unmanageable life of increasing uncertainty.

Why was Timothy McVeigh convicted of blowing up the Murra Federal Building? What motivated that act against children, against welfare recipients, against people filling out forms for other people? Did the clerks in the Federal offices do anything to McVeigh—or even to any of his self-defined "causes?" Or did they merely come to work because those were the jobs they could find? Does blowing up innocents help causes or is it just another step in a chain of social mutation?

This book is not about Charles Darwin's theories, but the whole idea of chance mutation and survival of the fittest makes us wonder—what is causing our social mutations—and what mutations are "fit" to survive? Is any of these violent social shifts a step toward survival—or is each step just random. Do these mutations have any pattern or is our society just unravelling?

Some professional basketball players have been "suspended for life" four or five times. Criminal behavior is a nuisance in professional sports—a nuisance—but not a crime. Once upon a time—in a fairy tale world—many professional athletes were admired because they stood for excellence and hard work. A professional sports mutation occurred—a mutation that reflects our larger social mutation.

Nightmares
Social mutation—chaos and collapse—when?

In mid-1997 the U.S. Army gave the LA Police Department 100 automatic weapons to match firepower with criminals. When cities need help from the Army to maintain law and order, how close is social collapse?

Milwaukee—Summer, 1995—tens of thousands were infected with cryptosporidium from an outdated, overstressed water supply. How close is social collapse?

Together, we may be re-writing the poem on the Statue of Liberty

Let us send you our tired, our poor,

Our huddled masses yearning to breathe something more,

The wretched refuse of our littered shore,

Our homeless, tempest-tossed

Yearning to leave through our corroding door!

How near are urban militias to operating large neighborhoods in LA, New York, Milwaukee, Philadelphia, Kansas City?

How soon will the local street security provided by these private armies seem better than the random crimes and beatings people fear in our cities?

Chaos—a scenario

Consider a scenario (not a prediction) of what could happen in a social breakdown.

As militias struggle for recognition and power, the Administration cuts off welfare and aid to militia members. Desperate for cash, the militias begin to "tax" locals. At first, people resist, but a combination of force and gradually safer streets convinces people that some law and order is better than what they have had. Meanwhile, local tax revenues decline.

At some point, militias rule in neighborhoods and cities provide basic services—but almost only in the daytime. People are fairly safe in their own areas, but are afraid to cross into other areas after dark. An informal "curfew," once intended for children and teens now rules everybody.

Entertainment centers (production studios) move offshore or concentrate in isolated "secure areas," where security is provided in three different ways—

    weakened public police

    friendly local militias,

    private security forces.

Urban people pay for piped-in entertainment, woven full of cues on what to buy and what to do next (a new form of NOW behavior "on command"—where "command" consists of sophisticated mixes of motivation and subliminal suggestion). On one recent TV show {9/30/97}, a "stupid blonde" was spouting off to the family about what was going on, and her next line was "and for dessert 'coytess'"—a convenient but transparent mispronunciation of "coitus." The entertainment industry is already essentially autonomous of cultural influence, and it is rapidly chipping away the residual stability of the tottering system. Large cities have become "money farms" for entertainment syndicates.

The entertainment industry is already powerful enough to be one of three major forces in a new "separation of powers" replacing the frayed system of executive, legislative, judicial. The former separation of powers—executive, legislative, judicial—crumbles away. A **new** triple set of powers could emerge as: urban militias; entertainment syndicates; private basic services.

State governments could become ghost operations, with the Federal Government collecting what revenues it can, primarily for two purposes—

    1. to fund (and thus, partially control) military operations, and

2. to keep the militias divided in order to prevent a militia-engineered coup against the Federal Government.

Entitlement programs and services for health or education slow down or stop as funding dries up.

Environmental programs are dropped. Education is mostly private, ad hoc, and local. Education is a mix of indoctrination and a few useful skills. Few people are educated beyond sixth grade.

Medical service is minimal and is privatized because no money reaches public services. Health standards drop, and death rates rise among children, pregnant women, new mothers, babies, and older people.

Rural areas become fortress areas, organized to keep unhappy urban people from migrating and destroying the remaining quality of life. Rural people fear militias and crime and reject all outsiders except known people or locally-meaningful groups. Small towns and small town residents are accepted as rural and reinforce rural isolation from cities.

The country lurches toward poverty, illness, and hunger. A few border areas try to join Canada or Mexico. Parts of New England and a few Mountain States organize into loose federations and, without a formal declaration of their independence, become *de facto* autonomous regions.

In this wildly disturbing scenario of social breakdown, the U.S.A. would exist more in name than in fact.

A world power vacuum could permit growing tensions between a few major power groups, primarily Western Europe, China, and nuclear-weapon-rich Russia.

Skilled Americans of every description might leave to where they would likely be accepted—blacks to fairly stable areas which would welcome well-educated black immigrants—countries such as South Africa—skilled whites to European countries which might accept them—skilled Asians to Asian homelands.

Hawaii's isolation could lead it rapidly toward nationhood. Hawaii could seek to consolidate the nuclear submarine fleet to guarantee its security. The nuclear submarine fleet is a major military power, even by itself. Hawaii is small enough to leverage its strengths. Its unique status gives it access to outside supplies and materials it needs.

America's largest cities would move into violence, conflict and chaos—similar to what happened in Ethiopia in the 1980s and the Congo, Bosnia, and Albania in the 1990s and new areas in the new century.

The loose pieces which would still call themselves the U.S.A. might wonder whether to split into tiny militarized "militia-kingdoms" or to try to regain unity and stability by looking for a new Stalin or Hitler to make them "great" again, the way the U.S.A. was "great" at the end of both World Wars, at the end of the Gulf War in the early 1990s, or at the first landing on the Moon.

End of a nightmare scenario

The nightmare scenario outlined above is not likely, but not impossible. It reminds us that *control* of what happens next is always challenging and may be nearly impossible if the pre-conditions are shaped by impulse-driven behavior without any traceable pattern.

Before dismissing the nightmare scenario completely, consider the Spanish Civil War and the terror in Argentina and Somalia. Consider Germany and Russia in the 1920s and 1930s, France in the 1790s. Examine the Cultural Revolution in China and Yugoslavia after Tito.

The American Civil War and the lynchings of the 1920s and 1930s occurred at a time when America thought it had a culture. What might happen when our culture is gone completely?

Ireland and Britain are social and cultural neighbors to the U.S.A. The intersection of these two societies and cultures in Northern Ireland is like a possible preview of a cultureless America.

At the beginning of the 21st Century, we cannot predict what will happen between now and 2025, but by that time the line between wild nightmares and reality could become blurry, at best.

Chapter 10

NOW—A NEW AMERICA

America is new all over again—*Gone with Another Wind*

We live in a new America. A blur of headlines obscures what's *really* changed.

The headlines keep us from thinking about change. It's the "trees and the forest." TV and newspapers "spam" us with endless stories about "trees" and we never notice that we are in a different "forest."

The "trees" are elections, crimes, explosions, trials, impeachments, scandals, celebrity deaths, Super Bowls. The new "forest" is a new society.

If we assume we're in the society we lived in a few years ago, we "think by old rules" and the lead stories are sensational. When we recognize we are in a new society, we see that many of the "sensations" or "outrages" are simply the way our new society actually is.

Society has changed and our culture is irrelevant to our society.

We describe society and culture in special ways, not strictly like the dictionary, but to explain the new America. We want to understand how Americans *escaped from time* and left the old culture behind. That culture was based on continuity over time, but we live instant by instant—apart from continuity—apart from time as it was once understood.

Society has *already changed* and culture will eventually conform to the way we live NOW because the way we lived ONCE is gone. It's time to write another "Gone with the Wind."

This go-around is changing *all* of America, not just the Old South described in "Gone with the Wind." A bigger wind is blowing in the 21st century.

Escape from Time describes why generations separated by just a few years are foreigners to one another.

During the 1980s and 1990s there were complaints about new immigrants, but we hardly noticed that Gen X grew up as immigrants in the Baby Boom world—and that Gen Y is a new group of immigrants shaping society at the beginning of a new century. We don't really need to be amazed when Gen Z seems to be from another galaxy.

These three "alphabet generations' (ever notice that they earned the *last* three letters and not A, B, C?) share one thing. They are the first generations born into the *Escape from Time.* The three are different from each other, but the chasm between them and everyone before them is huge.

Escape from Time is a cultural guidebook to a new culture being born at the beginning of Millennium Three. This new birth is not caused by switching dates from 1xxx to 2xxx. For our new society and our emerging culture, the date change is a coincidence—a reminder of other change.

Like the long-ago Civil War, *another wind* is blowing. A hurricane already shredded traditional society. And the abandoned baggage—the culture of that society—is blowing away piece by piece—right NOW!

That's the story told by *Escape from Time.* It's not a novel because it's not about someone else. This is *our* story.

Transition

A the beginning of a new millennium, we are somewhere between two states of mind:

I   **An old culture is ending**
a.   Existing laws have less effect
b.   New laws lag economic, technological and social change
c.   Pristine areas recede
d.   Institutions change; many traditional or formal institutions fade completely: Going, going, gone—bridge clubs, bowling, "old country" ethnic societies. Fourth generation Americans have blended backgrounds and don't identify with "the old country." For them, "There is no *there* there!"
e.   "Structural validation" of the individual loses its staying power. Awards are transitory.
f.   Social agendas are fading (except to meet the rich and famous—one agenda that never seems to die. The rich and famous of NOW society are different—entertainment hero replaces "dignitary.") "Missions" (supporting the symphony, fighting polio) have a short-term focus. Each "mission" is a new one-time event—a march, a benefit concert, a raffle.

II   **A new culture is being born**
a.   Action-based culture supersedes institutional culture
1.   Entertainment is delivered through the media
2.   Entertainment media and accompanying hype open the door to a menu of less than rational behaviors: smoking, fast-food eating habits, fad diets, drugs, violence.
b.   "Rapid Reach" focus. People emphasize reaching anyone anywhere. Cell phones and portable computers invade private spaces. A mother tells an adult son that his cell phone at the dinner table is rude. He ignores her "old fashioned ideas." Family intimacy vanishes.

c. Internet everywhere—all the time.

d. "Sliver Slices." People inhabit sliver slices of society as part of small, scattered "in groups." Sliver slices are based on any sort of orientation toward life—pro sports, single issue focus, pets, video poker, ATVs, RVs, PCs, fringe groups of right or left, religion, a subset of technology. One person's "in group" is another person's definition of "space cadet," "nerd," "gang member," "airhead," or "dummy."

e. Microgroups, scattered groups, shifting groups. Fluidity replaces stability. The ancient Greek philosopher, Heraclitus, who said "the only constant is change," would celebrate the fluidity of NOW society.

f. Live entertainment as "worship." Live entertainment is an all-encompassing experience. Entertainment meets our human need for transcendence. It centers our attention totally beyond self. Live entertainment re-runs the orgiastic mystery rites of ancient Greece.

g. Urge to "be known" drives irrational behaviors:

1. Activity is our mission in NOW society. The activity might be doing something "just to do it" like ATV outings, motorcycle rallies, sky-diving, mountain climbing, base jumping. People run up huge credit card debts to be able to say, "I did it."

2. External validation, e.g., travel as self definition—"I am where I've been."

3. Man crosses ocean in a small rowboat

4. "The one with the most toys wins"

5. "Human fly" climbs Sears Tower

6. Personal validation comes from whatever contemporary norm is dominant. Experience becomes "what is recognized:" running a marathon, going to Nepal or polluting Antarctica in the name of "the environment," taking a cruise, spending a week in "the big city," going to a concert—rock or country or symphony—

depending on whose validation I want. Doing what is "recognized," doing whatever provides my external validation determines what I will do next. What I have experienced determines who I meet next, where I go next. "Experience is destiny" in NOW society.

h. Outrunning the law. In time-sequence culture, there were always some people on the run from the law. NOW action is accelerated beyond norms and laws. Norms are "out of date." There is a cultural "red shift"—away from the past, and the gap is growing wider. While activity is speeding up, legal delays based on technicalities multiply and laws become a farce. In a backward sense, our laws are "outslowing" social change.

The upside of NOW society

The families of most Americans came from other places. American life shows little evidence of the way of life of the Americans who lived here before Europeans came. African Americans are descended from people brought here forcibly. They were ripped from their traditional society and forced to form a new society in the Old South. They formed still another society after the Civil War and another in-between society before Rev. Dr. King pointed the way to paralleling and blending into a larger American whole. Along the way NOW society was born, so African Americans, Native Americans, European Americans, Latino Americans, and Asian Americans are ALL in a new society.

NOW society is based on speed. Get it now—whatever it is: political power, fame, wealth, championships, promotion, sex, economic domination, military might, clothing, cruises, sport utility vehicles, sport cars, fast boats. Nothing waits in our NOW world.

American society of past-present-future told poor parents, "Get your children educated and they will be middle class. Their children will get a better education and they can go anywhere, do anything."

NOW society sends thousands of messages every day, "*You* can have it all right NOW!"

NOW people make incredible progress. Internet billionaires under age 30 and sporting multimillionaires under 30 and entrepreneurs starting their third or fourth business before age 35 have all done it. Teenagers sign huge entertainment contracts. Some entertainers are famous *before* they are teenagers. NOW people living in NOW society create wealth and products and breakthroughs. Economists were amazed at the boom of the 1980s, astonished at the bigger boom of the 1990s, and they have no models with which to comprehend the opening of the 21st Century.

Let's not bore ourselves with all the numbers. We have seen them on TV, read them in the press, heard them while driving. Our success is incredible.

We can break our own arms patting ourselves on the back—and we have earned it.

The downside of NOW society

Everyone in NOW society wants it right NOW. What is "it?" You know the list: political power, fame, wealth, championships, promotion, sex, economic domination, military might, clothing, cruises, sport utility vehicles, sport cars, fast boats. Not everyone gets "it." And many of us can't imagine that we will get "it"—certainly not when we want it—NOW.

We work under stress levels never experienced outside of wartime or slavery or a police state—all because we think we are coming closer to "it." But the target moves. We are living toward a moving target. Some of us crack when it seems hopeless. There's another list—not a pretty list:

alcohol

robbery   —   or murder—to get a few pieces of "it"

revenge	—	back to the old job after getting fired because you didn't get "it" *for them* quick enough
	—	back to the old job to shoot some of "them"
revenge	—	back to school with weapons because "they" took your girl friend—your dignity
drugs	—	use drugs and feel good right NOW
drugs	—	sell drugs and get more stuff
suicide	—	all these lies will stop right NOW
a new religion—		*these* new people have all the answers
gangs	—	somebody else is like me and together we'll get more stuff and we'll get our enemies
hate—		"they" are my problem—especially if they *look* different
rage—		"I can't take it any more." On the highway, in an airplane, in a supermarket line, anywhere
	—	and another person "cracks." No one knows what will happen when rage takes over.

The downside list is as long as the upside list. What's the line about no free lunch? Should it read, "A bigger lunch at any cost?"

NOW society will finally run out of gas. No society is eternal. Three possibilities:

1. NOW will evolve into something even newer because every society carries its own genes for change,
2. or—NOW society will self-destruct,
3. or—*someone* will say, "Enough NOW" and lead us in another direction. That person will be *our* Leif Erickson, *our* George Washington, *our* Einstein, *our* Rev. Dr. King of One More New America.

Consider how NOW will change into something else.

Genes for change

NOW society carries its own genetic code for change.

As NOW Society matures, and as it fosters its own culture, dominant patterns will form. These new patterns could shift very rapidly.

As the shredded moorings to the old culture fall away, NOW society will spawn its own loosely knit cultural fabric. The odds of extremism will rise—because extremes thrive on emotion, often emotion directed against a single target. NOW society focuses on rapid action. A bias toward rapid action could amplify extreme action and provoke an easy shift to absolutism.

Barriers to violent internal social conflict disappear when formal cultural mechanisms lose influence.

An era of plenty nourished the NOW society with its *throw-away* mentality. NOW society is not motivated to conserve. Single-use material fits our "discard mentality." We have divorced old restraints against waste.

Free of outmoded constraints NOW society will not be closely identified with *any* identifiable culture—*not even its own culture.*

The Internet is powering NOW society into rapid maturity. Splinter subsocieties have been forming from the birth of NOW society. High-speed communication accelerates the formation of splinter subsocieties.

Unnamed subsocieties pass each other like "ships in the night." They have no common reference points, no commonalities among groups. Very few people actually contact the whole range of fringe elements across the spectrum from "redneck" to populist to libertarian to Nazi to stereotypical "old-maid librarian," to hard-line Communist, or "old bachelor bookkeeper." When we encounter bizarre new forms of crime, we are amazed that these fringe lives are "right next door."

"Internet culture" (initially with unwritten rules, then gradually shaped by formal rules and new laws which never catch up with events) changed as rapidly as the equipment and software of the

Internet. The Internet began in a Defense Department environment. That "defense culture" was followed by a university and research culture. Then came early commercialization (a few entrepreneurs created "shareware" or free portals—and asked for voluntary payments). While early "break-even" commercialization struggled, there was an interlude of "freestyle, anything goes" on the Internet. The next stage of Internet culture was security-oriented and profit-centered with a struggle for control among several forces, including: service providers, users, content providers, signal carriers, advertisers, and regulators. All this took place in approximately half of one biological generation.

Consider the so-called "hackers." Within ten years that group went from being admired to being outlaws. The behavior of the average hacker did not change much during those ten years. Society's use of the Internet changed and a newer Internet culture was needed. When "hackers" first surfaced, the Internet was an electronic "Wild West." A decade later, big corporations depended on the internet. Military organizations used the Internet for control instead of simply information exchange. "Hackers" went from "creative freelance geniuses" to "nuisances" to "criminals." It's hard to remember that in the early 1990s "hacker" was a sort of grudging compliment, because in the early 21st Century "hacker" often means "criminal." "Internet society" changes every couple of years, and "Internet culture" follows one or two years behind. Whoever stands still for three years is in a different place, maybe a different world.

The broader society expropriates (and appropriates) property and ideas at will. Encroachment on individuality nudges some people to act as "lords," using force. They expropriate what they can and defend whatever they can control. Past-present-future thinking sees these local "lords" as gang leaders (and perhaps they are), but their "gangs" cannot exist unless people around them look sideways because their activities don't feel any worse than other social "warts."

Some everyday activities have so many warnings and caution labels and waivers imposed by outdated legal structures that NOW people can hardly wait for the old to disappear completely. Have you driven a new vehicle lately? The driver confronts a sea of warning signs and costly mandated disclaimers. Safe driving is secondary to reading black and yellow caution signs and black and white info sheets plastered around the vehicle. These placards are designed to establish new levels of control in a society which is splintering apart faster than it can institute more controls.

Violence and justice in NOW society

The strong push for gun control is less a deep desire to restrain violence than a subconscious social wish to stop the splintering—to maintain an older order while the people want to "do it my way." There is a non-stop rear-guard action against increasing "vigilante" tendencies. Our ossified "justice" system moves so slowly that, increasingly people will not wait. People are in the midst of discarding the justice system because it no longer works.

"Justice" is metamorphosing into "Whoever acts first is right by default."

The 1999 apprehension of a former adherent of the Symbionese Liberation Army (SLA) created an uproar. After more than 20 years of flight from the law ending in a half-million dollar home far from where the SLA operated, the "fugitive" was arrested. Neighbors said that the wealthy fugitive was "OK" by their standards.

Whatever happens to that person as a result of long-ago SLA activity may not even matter. The case demonstrates what people already know—"Slow law is no law!"

The motto, "Slow law is no law," is in sharp focus in NOW society. The so-called Symbionese Liberation Army was an aspect of NOW. The SLA operated by its own law, killed when it chose, and used violent tactics because it recognized that the old social paradigms were fading. However, in the 1970s the old institutional "culture" was alive enough to pursue the SLA and other groups looking to establish a new force, perhaps a dictatorship of their choosing. Vague guidelines rationalized their violence toward others—including innocent bystanders. No one can calculate the social costs had one of those groups prevailed.

In the full-blown NOW society which is emerging, rationalization is not needed. Lingering remnants of time-bound society and its culture are *more disturbing* to NOW people than to violent radicals of the 1970s. Those groups were immersed in a society and a culture, which *we* see as fading—but we have the benefit of 20/20 hindsight. Even though that society of past-present-future was already dying in the 1970s, it was not yet dead, and its established culture still held power firmly.

At the birth of Millennium Three, NOW people see the remnants of American past-present-future society as "ghosts." For a small, paranoid, and radical minority any hint of the return of that society threatens who they are. For them, the old culture is a menace—with its values, with its religious emphasis on "eternity," and with its institutions—schools, churches, even cemeteries as reminders of the past.

Extreme NOW people are hostile to bearers of tradition, government, courts, churches, —even cemeteries. NOW people have committed serious acts of violence in attacking old-line institutions. Schools and churches are easy targets. For extreme NOW people institutions represent a despised and faded past. Tradition is a terrible threat.

Extreme NOW society acts on the idea that "Quick law is the only REAL law." The old culture cannot turn back the new mood because the old culture is paralyzed by inaction. Laws and judicial decisions for "justice" have piled so high that there is no justice. The passing culture foretold the death of its justice system in its own maxim, "Justice delayed is justice denied."

Post-NOW society

Time-bound and analytical American society paved the way for its own slow death. No society is eternal. NOW society carries its own "genes for change"—even as it is emerging from a dissolving older society.

NOW society will age. It will grow old because its people will age. NOW behavior will eventually seem out of date and old fashioned and even "stupid" to another generation. The genes for change are at work in NOW society before it reaches its own maturity.

How long will it take for NOW society to lose its vigor—to seem old? Perhaps only one or two decades, perhaps half a century. Social change is so rapid that three or four decades would be a long lifetime for NOW society. Seeds of change for NOW society are already sprouting—loss of environmental resiliency and a fragile infrastructure. Services are necessary in a modern society—water systems, for example. Delivery of these services depends on the fragile and highly-stressed infrastructure.

Good water systems are needed to maintain public health. No civil society can function without a healthy population. NOW society is not motivated to maintain what exists. NOW society wants to DO something much more than it wants to KEEP something. If NOW society produces institutions to maintain existing structures it will stop looking like NOW society and look like it is reverting to a past-present-future mindset.

If older structures of society begin to re-emerge, NOW society will suffer a sort of schizophrenia. The discredited institutions of a passing society are not acceptable as part of a newly forming NOW culture.

Very likely a "post-NOW" society will emerge to throw away the loosely knit culture which is the only culture truly in tune with NOW society. By 2040 NOW behavior will be fringe behavior—and oddly enough probably the fringe behavior of "old people."

NOW living thoroughly rejects whatever went before.

Get a life!

More, me, now!

It's all here now. There's nothing "out there…then!"

NOW society is not as absolute as NOW people might intuitively believe. Successor generations often reject "what went before."

Rapid reach

To the two generations of analysts, "traditionalists" were "slow plodders." NOW people laugh at the empty lives of analysts—lives which seem frozen away from all motion or change.

Gen X-ers see more in life than the slow progression in the lives of Baby Boomers. Gen X is idealistic and assertive all at the same time, and Gen X escaped from time—altogether. Gen X grew up in a society for which "time" is not a useful concept. "Time" is a living fiction to Gen X. Time is a handy yardstick for sequencing events and for measuring psychological movement between events. For Gen X 1999 happened, then 2000 happened, then 2001, etc. "So what?" Gen X is a NOW generation because the broader social escape from time was already underway while Gen X was maturing.

Gen Y did not need to escape from time. Gen Y grew up with an entertainment culture all around them. They don't want to leave that setting because it feels natural to them. Like Gen X, Gen Y grew up apart from time. Gen Y has no interest in re-entering time. The traditional passage of time is a vague and distant concept associated with petrified parents and with funny old patriotic, sentimental grandparents. In this respect Gen Y is in tune with Gen X.

Gen Z is too young to know it's a unique generation. Gen Z is the first generation to live outside of time *and* outside of geography. Geography implies a "there" and a "here." For Gen Z there is no "there." It's all here. Distant places are near and "foreign" people live next door. Gen Z is immersed in an expanding "rapid reach" world. Formal geography is unimportant. If a Gen Z person has trouble finding India on a globe or can't repeat "facts" about India, this "shortcoming" is not really relevant because there is probably a classmate or a neighbor from India (or from Thailand or Africa or wherever)—someone who knows what the "distant" place is really like. In any case, Gen Z knows how to ask a computer where to find any country or almost anything at all.

Everywhere is within the scope of "rapid reach." There are no geographic boundaries in the psychological world of Gen Z. If we look at traditionalists, analysts, NOW people, and the three "alphabet generations" (X, Y, Z) which were immersed in NOW from their beginning, we understand that what seem like successive generations of Americans are almost foreigners to each other.

These tightly-packed successor generations do borrow from their predecessors, only vaguely aware that they are mimicking fragments of lifestyles they have openly disowned. They borrow because no generation creates everything new, not because they want to repeat what they reject.

Social uncertainty principle

Even though transgenerational borrowing is significant, society is changing so rapidly that it is not merely pulling away from traditional norms. In spite of transgenerational borrowing, society discards temporary yardsticks which might be used to gauge change. We cannot even measure the pace of change because there is so little relationship between what happened and what is happening and what will happen.

We live in a "Social Uncertainty"—like the world of physics described by Heisenberg's Uncertainty Principle. Rephrased to fit society, the Uncertainty Principle says, "We can know where we are or we can know how fast we are changing, but cannot simultaneously know both."

If we stop to see where we are, the world around us has changed. If we observe how quickly society is changing, we lose track of where we are. It's a bit like being in a car: if you look through the windshield, you read the road signs and know where you are. If you look out the side window, you see trees and buildings flashing by and realize how fast you are moving. We need to use maps and speedometers to do both—and then we miss the places we are driving through. If we do that, we are analysts, not NOW people.

Our social application of Heisenberg's Uncertainty Principle does not say that we cannot know *anything*. The Social Uncertainty Principle says that we can't be scientific about what we know and how things are changing because we are part of what we are measuring. We affect what goes on. One person in isolation has *almost* no effect, so that one person might make a sort of objective judgment about society (this objective judgment would also be completely subjective), but if *many* of us agree to discuss how we are changing, we start to affect what's changing. It's not "bad" that society is affected by our discussions. Maybe it's even "good" if that happens. Perhaps discussion produces "good change," not "bad change."

I hope that this book does change how we are changing. You (reader) can see that I'm not a NOW person. I'm not "disapproving" of NOW, and I don't "approve" NOW. NOW doesn't need me, but maybe what you (reader) and I (author) can do is to help NOW people recognize why the "old stuff" around them feels so outdated and uncomfortable. It's not "bad" not to fit, not "bad" for NOW people, not "bad" for traditional people or analysts. It's just how our society is.

NOW people live in a world changing like no other "world" has ever changed. NOW people are living out a huge experiment in replacing an outmoded world. They can use every bit of help available—especially if it's not criticism or even praise—but just a mirror to look at their lives in a new way.

Traditional people and analysts can use this book as a telescope looking ahead. What they will see is a brilliantly changing galaxy—a new society which they might as well enjoy, because it's arriving NOW!

NOW society self-destructs—a possibility

The range of possible self-destruct modes of NOW society is nearly endless. A few examples show how self-destruction *could* occur. Self destruction is not likely, but it shouldn't be laughed off as impossible.

America might spend itself into such a huge international debt position that other countries "call in their chips." If that happens, nobody will want dollars and we won't be able to afford things we depend on—foreign oil, clothing from almost anywhere, special items not manufactured here. Domestic dissatisfaction could trigger riots and might invite a military takeover.

The gap between haves and have-not could grow so large that millions follow new religions or new leaders or vote for a party so radical that the country is torn apart.

We could become so accustomed to luxury that we "get soft" and outside groups simply take over.

New technologies might make it possible for a small group to bring down the government. Computer hackers have penetrated far into command and control software, and no "fix" has stopped them.

"Enough NOW!"—a leader shows us a better way

NOW society *might not* evolve into something new. It could self-destruct. Or—some leader might convince people that there is an even better way—a way to live without the pressures of NOW life.

We know that every society carries a "genetic code" which will eventually lead to another society. Nobody will ever understand *how* a "code for change" is embedded in society. "Genetic change" is not "easy change." After NOW society develops its own culture to replace both the faded American time-based culture and the "half-alive" culture of the analysts, not many people will want to digest another new culture.

While NOW culture is still maturing in the dominant NOW society, a leader could emerge and ask people, "Is getting more of 'it'—getting more 'stuff' worth the stress we live with, the rage, the revenge, the hatred?"

This kind of new leader can come from anywhere—or just about from "nowhere." She or he could be nearly holy or nearly demonic. He or she could be frighteningly rational or might lead through sheer emotion. However this person (group) leads, he or she (they) will take us where we've never been before. We can't go back, but we can borrow from where we have been.

What needs to happen? For "peaceful change" away from NOW, we need to slow down. NOW leaders are NOW people with great skill, great education and occasionally great luck. NOW leaders have built our fabulously wealthy society—without intending a downside. The unintentional downside is there. We are a rage-filled society. We are stressed out.

In some ironic way, curing the problems of NOW living—of NOW society—involves slowing down, breaking the cycle. NOW life is exhilarating. It's fun. Not everyone is participating in the "good side of NOW." People who do participate pay a different kind of price than people left out, but they do pay a price. They live with more and more frustrated, rage-filled people. Even the "winners" are "neighbors of rage."

Americans search for peace—for themselves: mountain cabins, wilderness lodges, "rent an island," "buy an island," vacation on a remote farm in Tuscany where the nearest village conversation might focus on which village's wine (naturally, their own is best) is "almost as good as ours," stay home on Sunday and do nothing (even a worship service is too much), rent a beach villa, meditate, climb a mountain— at least the people you meet are too tired to talk about anything but the mountain,—

As long as we return to the "contest" on Monday morning, the villa, the mountain, even the meditation, are forgotten in the rush of the commute. Turn on the car radio; listen.

"Is the Eisenhower jammed? Should I aim for the Kennedy? Which bridge has an accident? Is the Santa Monica plugged? Is there a breakdown on BART?"

"Blast! Oil is up. The internet stocks are likely to open lower."

"What will our crazy governor do next? Give an interview to the Inquirer? Open a nudist camp for defeated politicians?"

"I can't believe how much debt these guys are assuming in the takeover. Thank God I'm almost at the office. What happened to the weekend?"

Think it's different for a day laborer? Guess again.

"Who'll sit with the girls Wednesday? I work late and the wife works at three. One sitter has classes. The other wants cash. Payday is Friday. Next week is worse.

"Better add antifreeze when I get home. Can't fix the radiator leak until Saturday."

Entertainment; escape; getting through the week; short on sleep; antacid; pain reliever; antidepressant; coffee nerves. At least there's "office casual." Another joke—the leisure suit of the post-Y2K era. Anything to distract us from our pace. The "sandwich generation" is now the "wrap generation." Eat a wrap on the run. Sandwiches have tops and bottoms. The wrap generation is rolled up in it all—all the time! "Grab and go" is a *faster food* slogan—because *fast food* is too slow.

Just maybe a leader will jump out of nowhere. Maybe there will be a slowdown. Was Falun Gong (Falun Dafa) an accident for China? Or is it their people's way of saying, "Too much?" A different kind of "too much," but still more than they could handle.

Can we break out of NOW society without crashing or without waiting for genetic social change which can't be avoided? Do we have a choice? There are three ways out: genetic change (social genetics, not human genetics) to something different; self destruct; choice—a different path, a different pace.

What kind of choice is there? The choice will be simple.

The price will be to lose some of the gains: power, wealth, dominance,—

The gain will be to free ourselves from drugs, alcohol, hate, rage,—

Not every problem will go away. No "golden age" is waiting because someone says, "Do this!" If we break out of NOW, other choices are out there. Those choices might be made apart from rage and inner pressure, with less stress and more companionship.

Unless we choose, or until we crash and self-destruct, we will be NOW people moving toward an exciting, unknown, and tough future—faster and faster.

Postscript—getting a life—a second time

NOW society is a powerful attraction. Marketing and advertising use highly researched techniques to sell the attractions we have called "it" and "stuff." A leader who offers a "*slow down*" alternative will be laughed at, called unbalanced, ignored. Still—there are millions who can't keep up and other millions who are tired of the pace. If the choice is clear and the challenge is clear, people might choose a different pace. The first NOW generation said "get a life." The pace of "getting a life" might look like too much of something else to Gen X, Gen Y, and Gen Z. They might be ready—especially if they internalize the costs of NOW.

A new leader will be simple, skilled, and persistent—and not in a hurry.

PART FOUR

RECONFIGURING

Chapter 11

Beyond NOW

"We are not yet what we are becoming!"

Almost 500 years ago, Martin Luther wrote those words about becoming more than we have already become.

America *is* becoming more than we have been. We could look on changes in America as coming clouds of doom and gloom, but why? Change means losing something old, gaining something—perhaps many things—new.

America is growing out of its old culture, leaving behind the pilgrim ethic. We are becoming people of science and pragmatism. We DO things. We don't contemplate the meaning of actions. We simply act.

Americans refuse to be guided by an older cultural inheritance. The old culture is torn apart by "NOW" living.

NOW people live on the frontier of behavior. NOW actions don't wait for rules. NOW actions take us where there are no rules.

Some of NOW is applauded by many. Some of NOW creates cries of outrage from many.

The cheering section is loud when former dictators are tried under laws that were dreamed up after the fact. The boos are deafening when existing laws are applied to popular people.

Americans create rules along the way and apply the rules when they feel right.

Huge gains are made in science because scientists are cheered when they move beyond yesterday's rules, yesterday's laws:

+ Research into cloning will build body parts for people destroyed by disease or injury

+ Forward leaps in health care are pushing back the meaning of "old"

+ Jack Kevorkian has redefined the meaning of lifelong suffering—if life is only suffering, it ought to come to a quick end. "It" is the suffering—even if shortening "it" means ending life.

+ During heat waves we run air conditioners in public spaces to keep the elderly cool, even though we are almost certain that every time we use more energy, the atmosphere heats up more—that we are creating conditions for worse heat waves next year and other years after that—for other people who will be elderly then.

+ We run nuclear generators and fight about where to put the spent nuclear fuel.

+ Transgenic research puts human genes into mice.

+ Researchers are beginning to design tailor-made super people—one gene at a time. When we can boost several genes separately, we will learn how to boost them in a group. Super people will come slowly at first, then faster.

+ Part-human, part-animal beings will emerge from genetic inquiries looking into what is possible.

If you are outraged by some of the items in the list above, you're not alone—but you are wasting your outrage. These changes are symptoms—symptoms that our American society is moving beyond the culture it once inherited.

What is society? Society is a collection of actions by individual people and by groups of people. Society is what all of us do together—whether we act one person at a time or whether we do something we all planned together and agreed to do. Increasingly, society has no set of principles, no rules.

Why? The old rules were our culture, and we are divorcing ourselves from that culture.

We—Americans—were once in step with Pilgrim piety, with a Constitution shaped by the Enlightenment in Europe in the 18th century, with a civil culture shaped by the Bible and with the sense of ethics brought from Europe by millions of immigrants.

"Good-Bye, George. Good-Bye, Abe."

"Build a nation!"

"The business of America is business," Calvin Coolidge.

"Give me your tired, your poor,…," Emma Lazarus.

"…a nation dedicated to the proposition that all are created equal," Abraham Lincoln.

"We hold these truths to be self-evident—life, liberty, the pursuit of happiness," Thomas Jefferson.

America flourished on ideals for 200 years. For some, it was freedom, for some equality, freedom of speech, freedom of religion, opportunity through business, a refuge for the persecuted. This was America's culture.

Psychologically, NOW people are not able to think in terms of the culture of America. The increasingly NOW society has forgotten the ideals of America…not forgotten *deliberately*. Ideals are part of a *past*, but NOW has no past.

We are not in step with those things any more. We are tired of that culture and we are "getting a divorce" from it.

Many marriages end in divorce when people suddenly realize that the only tie left is the formal, legal bond called marriage. It's that way with our society and our culture. There's no longer any real relationship between the two—only a leftover sort of lip-service from another era.

In the earlier chapters of this book, we learned that the old culture doesn't relate to NOW people, and most of us are NOW people or we are becoming NOW people. We learned that the "social divorce" is already a done deal. We are ALREADY divorced from that old culture.

What Next?

NOW is *whatever comes next*, and "whatever comes next" might as well feel good. Otherwise, why should *anything* be next?

Ideals point to goals—goals in a future worth working for. When the future is gone, psychologically, *nothing* is worth working for. When the past disappeared, so did the future—*really*.

Beyond culture—only "happenings"

Sometimes people talk about a "future," but it's only a concept, like "e=mc². " Americans are sort of proud to quote Einstein's famous formula. Many people also know enough chemistry to say "H_2O" and feel proud of their "chemistry" background. It's that way with e=mc², and it's that way with "future." Almost everyone uses the word "future," but few *understand* it psychologically. We (at least NOW people) have disconnected from "future."

Every day more Americans are NOW people. Every day "future" seems more like an empty word. People say the word like they might say e=mc²—or some other "magic formula" which they don't understand, but it doesn't *do* anything for them (or *to* them).

Increasingly, time shrinks to NOW...to this instant and to what happens when "this" instant stops and another NOW happens.

No past, no future, no culture...just "happenings"—sort of reminiscent of "happenings" at an open house. You return from an open house, and someone asks, "Did anything happen?" You answer, "Not really," and yet, many "happenings" occurred. You bumped into a person from work. You met a telecom competitor, another fitness freak. You thought someone insulted you, but you weren't sure because it was too vague.

You answer, "Not really," because what did occur was just one thing after another, just more NOW happenings. Without context, we are living "not really" lives.

For a person accustomed to "happenings," "History" is sort of like visiting a "Hall of Fame" for sports heroes in a sport he/she never heard of.

Future is like science fiction without any plot—a serious, glitzy light show…impressive! Empty!

Then there is the "Look and Feel" of NOW—a society with no defined "culture"—a "No fault" society made up of disparate, unrelated happenings.

Consider the political scandals and investigations of the late 1990s:

Mr. Clinton, Whitewater, "Zippergate," Special Prosecutor, Mr Starr.

The NOW public couldn't care less about what really *did* happen. Everything was NOW stuff. It's OK, even if unusual things *did* happen, and it's OK if it *didn't*. "*Get yours*" rules! There's no vague, historical "duty of office" or "upholding a constitution."

It's all OK, no matter what your viewpoint, as long as "their guy" is being attacked, and I defend "my guy."

Psychologically, it's all NOW behavior. Fewer and fewer people care about what happened or if there might be some "objective results."

If Prosecutor Starr was carried away—beyond his assignment, that's just NOW behavior, not so bad, as long as "my guy" comes out OK and "their guy" gets the short end.

Temporarily, a new standard emerged. "It doesn't matter what 'he' did as long as no one lied about it." Another new standard: "He can investigate anything because he's a *special prosecutor*." For a NOW person, what comes *next* is special.

Does it matter?

A NOW story

A motorist, "Tim," hits a pedestrian, "Tonya," at an intersection in a megacity. Tonya lies in the road, unconscious, bleeding, and breathing such shallow breaths that she looks dead. A huge crowd gathers and starts blaming Tim for killing Tonya. Someone grabs Tim and starts to beat him and kick him for his crime. Soon Tim is dead—good revenge, swift justice in a NOW world.

Before the crowd melts away, "dead" Tonya revives and starts to get up. The crowd realizes that Tim was killed "unjustly" and blames Tonya. Tim was killed for something that didn't happen. It's Tonya's "fault" that Tim is dead. How can the crowd "fix" the injustice? Someone starts to beat Tonya. Before long she is dead. It was her "fault" that the motorist died for nothing.

There were no "accident" victims, only "NOW victims." This is a NOW culture.

The story of Tim, Tonya and the crowd seems preposterous, but it actually happened in another country, in a country where traditional village-based culture was wiped out by mobility to megacities.

What is the emerging "look" of NOW in America?

1. Business is increasingly transaction-based, decreasingly relationship-based
2. More social and business relationships are one-time arrangements—a "one-shot" society is emerging
3. New religions will proliferate
   a. Mystery-based cults
   b. Experiential cults—sometimes focusing on orgiastic behavior
   c. Guru-based cults

4. Spending on lifestyle will increase, though some "analysts" will save heavily, perhaps keeping the national savings rate from falling farther
5. The percentage of people with no assets will grow
6. Wealth will concentrate—especially land ownership; more people will find it easier to lease land—even to lease when they build
7. Reliance on the armed forces will increase—shifting from interdiction to control of unrest, etc.
8. Industrial security will increase
9. Subcultures will proliferate
   a. Survivalists
   b. Paramilitary militias
   c. Some gangs will evolve into paramilitary groups, some into cults, others into hybrids
10. Gated communities or quasi-secure areas will grow—new forms of "security" may be partly electronic, partly through private ownership of roads, partly through hybrid methods.

Strange new world

Aldous Huxley sketched a bizarre tech future in Brave New World and Orwell followed with all-seeing Big Brother.

Cybersociety makes their nightmares possible, but another world is already waking up—"Frag-world."

Frag-world begins when everyone follows a different NOW— "Things" *happen*—what happens is different for *every* person. A strange new fragmented world of NOW happenings is out there.

And still—even NOW people cluster. They sort of "bunch up" in little groups—one-shot, one-night, one-trip, "once-only" bunches. A few of these "bunches" find a comfort level and keep going.

"Bunches" go without plan, without anything but a comfort level, but suddenly, for a few, there's something magnetic—maybe a religious rush, maybe power—recognition? money? sex?—but mostly an experience of something bigger. That's how the strange new society is beginning.

Outlines of this emerging world are forming right now—as these words are being written and even later—as you are reading them.

Too long ago to remember, millions came from Europe in ships—to a New Society still forming, and something was built. New people adopted a growing culture. It was a New World, a Shining City on a Hill—a city long gone because the people who live in what *was* the city no longer remember the city. The Shining City is in a forgotten past.

The Shining City flourished, dazzled the world, attracted giants like Einstein and Solzhenitsyn and created heroes of science and entertainment and sports. The City created adventures—in the skies, in space, into the atom. The City analyzed the world—astrophysics, genetics, business empires. The City lived like no other. The City called people out of time into NOW.

The City helped people forget, and they DID forget. Where did the City come from? Where is the City going?

They forgot because NOW has no other dimensions. Don't ask, don't tell. Don't even pretend to *know*. The City taught so well that it could go away. All that's left is the lesson. NOW! Everything is NOW. Whatever happens next is the only thing. Once it was said that winning isn't everything, it's the *only* thing. How ancient! How quaint!

NOW is the only thing. No City. No memories. No thing after NOW—except another NOW. A succession of NOW happenings.

Critics of business said there was too much focus on the results of the next quarter. Ludicrous! Reports and rumors are weekly, daily, *hourly*.

This is the social soup for the growth of something never seen. Cybersociety without a vision is being born. There are no birth pains, because the birth just happens.

Certainly some people suffer from change. That's their worry. No one sees them. No one feels their pain. All they need to do to go without pain is to forget and then NOW is theirs!

Dredging around to connect with NOW

No past—nothing happened before *this*.
No future—nothing will happen after *this*.
If I do what I want now, I'll get what I want NOW.
Ever consider how sports reinforce the NOW way of living?

A football lineman jumps offside; a flag is thrown; the opposing team makes a decision and a penalty is walked off or declined; then the whole thing is over—perhaps some seconds ran off the clock. Maybe *no* time off the clock.

A baseball pitcher throws ball four and the batter trots down to first. A whole new situation is set up. The situation that *was* is gone and the next pitch has its effect *right now*—as soon as the pitch is thrown. Every pitch brings up a new NOW. A game of baseball is one NOW situation after another—little bits of action which look like one piece of cloth in a sports report, or maybe even in the box score, but each piece of action is really a new NOW situation.

In basketball, the shot-clock splits a game into a whole string of 24-second NOW situations. The shot-clock was introduced to set up a string of NOW situations—to end the famous "stall" which was part of basketball. Attitudes shifted and the "powers of the game" wanted action on a short timetable.

Bottom-line in industry shortens more and more frequently. Waste Management, a huge waste disposal firm, was bought out after four different CEOs were in charge for a grand total of eight months. Each new CEO had eight weeks to do something with the company. Can you guess what anyone could have done in eight weeks? Maybe learn the names of the office staff at headquarters? Learn where the coffee machines are?

An outmoded, analytical mind might say, "Give him (her?) time!" With NOW thinking in charge, only blind luck could possibly turn that huge company around in eight weeks. Bringing in a new CEO every eight weeks is laughable to analysts and to traditional thinkers.

In the context of NOW, no time horizon is too short—because *nothing* comes after NOW.

Without a context, no request, no demand is unreasonable. The quintessential NOW CEO is Al "Chainsaw" Dunlap, a business "has been," at least temporarily. When he walked in the door of a new company, heads rolled. Personnel cuts were made before thought began. The strategy worked because no one questioned quick action—especially because salary costs were slashed up front—and immediately.

"Chainsaw" strategy kicks in and NOW people see something happen. Huge charges for "restructuring" are shrugged off because SOMETHING is happening NOW.

The company is sold for a quick profit and everyone is "happy." The next owner deals with more restructuring costs and with a staff drained of motivation. No one wonders what the long-term outlook is because "long term" begins when the current backlog of orders runs out—a month, maybe two or three months ahead, but not right NOW.

Without a past, without a future, EVERYTHING is "one-shot," "once-around," "all-by-myself."

Interlude

Before we go farther, let's remember what we are doing in this book. We are *describing* what is happening as our society divorces its culture.

Our society grew away from culture when society lost touch with the past, when society no longer expected a future.

Some people (in other words, a portion of our society) still do expect a future, still feel connect to a past.

The some live in a present with a past and a connection to a future. Every day, the some are fewer, and the many (analysts and most especially NOW people) are more. This is how society is detaching from culture—one person at a time.

Culture "connects." *Society"* is in a "disconnecting" mode.

Culture from the top

In an empire with an absolute monarch or in a dictatorship with iron rule, some form of culture is imposed from the top down. The imposed culture is often linked with a formal ideology.

Where there has been emperor worship, as in ancient Rome or in Japan, ideology precedes an individual sovereign. The sovereign is an "embodiment" of the ideology.

In a dictatorship, ideology may precede a dictator—as communism preceded Stalin; it may come along *with* the person of the dictator, as in the case of Hitler and the Nazi ideology.

Occasionally, the only discernible ideology in a dictatorship is the *person* of the dictator, as it seems to be in Iraq with Saddam Hussein.

In cases of culture from the top—emperor worship, absolute monarchy, or dictatorship, "culture" is linked with the power of government. If government fails, the ideology which defined a "culture" for the society usually fails with the government, and a cultural vacuum results. Some examples of this phenomenon are: the lack of cohesiveness in Roman society after the Empire fell; the social collapse in France following the French Revolution and the guillotining of Louis XVI and Marie Antoinette; the floundering of Russian society when the last Tsar abdicated—until Communism became a new ideology for Russia, and 70 years later when Communism fell apart—Russian society again struggling to overcome a passing culture.

After Hitler fell, Germany was partially spared from a cultural vacuum—for two reasons: first the occupying powers quickly put laws in place; second, Nazi rule in Germany lasted only twelve years, so the records and collective memory of the earlier culture were available. When East Germany was re-united with the West, another "culture shock" resulted from the collision of two political cultures and from the shock of emerging NOW secularism which the "old" Germany had not experienced.

Theocratic rule is another type of top-down culture—based on beliefs about what God expects. Theocratic culture is capable of great endurance because theocratic culture *can readily* outlive a particular leader.

Western Europe developed into a theocratic culture after Rome fell to invading tribes in the 5th century, and the Western Church gradually asserted cultural dominance.

In the Middle East and North Africa, society was shaped by a different theocratic culture—Islam.

Islam and Christianity each defined a culture. In each case, society "knew" its roots. For each society the culture was deemed "worth dying for," and many people *did* die for their culture.

These theocratic cultures have been very resilient and the societies which "inhabit" these cultures lived in relative harmony with their cultures for 1000 years or more, but in the 21st century, societies—Islamic *and* Christian—are separating from their cultures.

Evidence of separation from culture in Western Society is everywhere. America, which was the quintessential Protestant culture, is as secular as the ancient Rome which was first "infected and affected" by Christianity. In Italy, where Roman Catholicism has some characteristics of a state religion, the birth rate is below replacement level in spite of repeated papal condemnation of birth-control.

Decades of killing and maiming in Northern Ireland make one wonder if there is anything of a common underlying Christian culture which links two separate "societies," Protestant and Roman Catholic.

Rapid social change began to undermine a newly-established theocratic order in Iran within twenty years. Theocratic culture began with great support from the masses, but the influence of NOW society quickly penetrated tight social controls and Iranian society is showing signs that NOW thinking might separate the society from theocratically imposed culture.

Turbulence

When masses of people attached themselves to the prevailing culture, society had an imprint of that culture. As people distance themselves farther and farther from the ostensibly prevailing culture—either by detaching themselves completely as NOW people have already done or by identifying with splintering subcultures, they may still pay lip service to the once dominant culture. The price of separating openly from the seemingly mainstream culture is to risk loss of status in the eyes of powerful social and economic elites whose favor might still be helpful—because there are rewards for people who "play the game." This suggests that the" social divorce," e.g., separation of society from the formal culture, is even more complete than surface appearances indicate.

Consider how people "pass through the courts" for "crimes"—actions which qualify as crimes within the ever-less-relevant "old culture"— "crimes" which are no longer crimes in the world of NOW. These "court transients" may express sorrow and remorse to lighten penalties imposed by courts, but the same people resume NOW patterns of behavior as soon as they are free from control of the courts.

Example: the return of "junk bond" profiteer Michael Milken to the financial arena after he served a jail term—even though he was technically forbidden to do so. The courts had to step in a second time to stop Milken from behavior which was supposedly "off limits" for him. Milken's new penalty, though substantial in most people's eyes was little more than a scolding for a man who amassed an earlier fortune in the junk-bond arena.

A football fable of NOW

Rapidly shifting loyalties in professional sports provide a backdrop for understanding NOW. Anyone who follows a major professional team sport, especially baseball, football, or basketball, is familiar with shifts in "loyalty."

Consider the following fictitious story about "Barry," a football player.

Barry was drafted in an early round by Team One. After contract wrangling and a short "hold-out," Barry signed a contract for more money than most of his college classmates would earn in an entire career. He hadn't even proven that he could play football at the professional level, but Barry was already wealthy as far as his friends and classmates were concerned.

Let's follow Barry's career. During the first year, he's pretty green and not yet ready for pro football except in mop-up situations at the end of a game. He spends the whole year on the bench. The team is "loyal" to him and it hopes for big things from Barry after he breaks in. In year two Barry plays fairly well. Year three Barry can't shake a moderate injury so he hardly plays at all. Finally, in the last year of his initial contract, Barry has healed and has mastered the pro game. He's well-coached and his natural talent gives him "rising star" status.

In the NOW era, Barry postures for a big contract throughout his entire fourth year. At the end of the season, Barry signs with Team Two for double what Team One paid him, but only 15% more than Team One offered him for a new contract. Barry has a press conference with Team Two to announce a new three-year contract. He received a large signing bonus and praises the new team's "commitment to winning." After the press conference, reporters ask Barry about Team One and

Barry criticizes Team One because "they don't really appreciate their players and never did give him the chance he deserved."

After two seasons with Team Two, Barry gets restless, refuses to extend his contract, threatens to refuse to play for "this low salary" and demands to be traded. Finally, Barry "suffers" through the third season with Team Two and then signs a contract with Team Three. New press conference, same tired line: "Team Three is really committed to winning. The coach really *cares* about his players. The owner is a 'class act' in this city."

When asked about Team Two, he "admits" that he misjudged" their commitment to winning and how the players were treated at Team Two. Barry praises the "new spirit" at Team Three. "They appreciate me," says Barry.

Meanwhile players from Team Two are saying the same things when they leave for Team One. Ditto Team Three players leaving for Team Two.

Pro football grew up in an era with different loyalties. People like Barry spent entire their entire career with Team One.

Society values paychecks NOW, featured playing status NOW, name recognition NOW. Pro players value the same things society values. Fans of any professional sport are familiar with the litany sung by NOW players. The NOW era has reduced loyalty to a single season—*maybe*!

Loyalty belonged to traditional culture, but we are in the process of trashing that culture. We don't value loyalty any longer because it does not fit NOW culture. The trashing of culture is a NOW phenomenon. It's not a deliberate trashing of culture—it's just that our society ignores what was its culture. For NOW society, "culture" is expendable.

NOW behavior is strongest among young people—especially Gen-X people and their younger companions. The physical demands of pro sports guarantee that players are young—mostly Gen-X with Gen-Y coming up.

It's no surprise that young, NOW people behave like NOW people. Why shouldn't they? It's what NOW people do!

This is not a criticism of athletes. Athletes are the "workers" of professional sports.

What about the managers—owners, coaches, etc? NOW behavior defines management in industry *and* in sports. The NOW phenomenon was given a big boost when corporations started fixating on results from the next quarter. Even a professional sports season is longer than the focus allowed to some corporate executives.

Every week thousands of job cutbacks of workers and managers are announced—mostly by large corporations. These companies are part of the NOW behavior phenomenon.

City of a Million Precincts

As NOW solutions spread from business into professional sports and are reflected back from sports into the everyday workplace, people are sorted into smaller and smaller groups—into groups with very temporary interests in common—until one day, the urban center is suddenly a "City of a Million Precincts."

When social patterns—once shaped by culture—are detached from their cultural pattern, society becomes more a "writhing tangle of people" and less an "orderly place to live."

In divorcing the patterns of culture, "society" is becoming a collection of "onesies" and "twosies."

An English poet laureate once wrote, "The center cannot hold." In NOW society, there IS no center.

What will the *City of a Million Precincts* look like when it shakes off its newness?

Spastic City—Fragmented World

On a Tuesday in March, 1998 all the news media trumpeted the tragedy of how two school boys shot four girls and a woman teacher that day. Four days later—even before the last funeral for the victims—a

Milwaukee newspaper headline blared that it was tough for Jonesboro to "Get over" the murders. Three days later a national radio newscast indicated that students were "coping" in the school cafeteria—"laughing and joking." Whatever the real feelings in Jonesboro, the media wanted to be done with the event so they could begin their "analysis."

The headline in the Milwaukee paper was a signpost telling us where we are. As soon as the NOW-ness of an event wears off, it's time to move on. To the newspaper headline writer and to the killers of four young girls, the girls will be forgotten—or an "unpleasant" reminder—long before the girls would have graduated from high school.

It happened "yesterday." Let's get on with NOW!

Shortly after a large corporation laid off a couple of hundred workers, the wife of the president of that company told me how "tiring" it was to hear the people complain. She said, "Why don't they get on with their lives?" Perhaps the underlying message was, "I don't want to hear about it I have other things on my agenda." When would the laid off workers and their families really be able to "get on with their lives." Perhaps a lot depends on how old the workers are—or depends on luck.

"Chuck" was one of those layoff casualties. Chuck handled his problem well and landed "on his feet." "Bill" was one of Chuck's "classmates" at a local outplacement center. Bill had been a salesman for another firm. Bill dressed for success—pressed suit, luxury car, all the toys. Bill told Chuck he was worried sick because he had huge mortgage payments due every month on his oversize house. The next payment was due in two weeks and Bill had no money in the bank. Bill's "run with the goodies" was over, and Bill was closing in on his 46th birthday. I lost track of Bill because his story was second-hand to me, but you can fill in your own set of details.

The sailors with Columbus worried about sailing off the end of the world in 1492. Bill *did* sail off the end of his world in the last two years of the 20th century.

The world is broken into little chunks. One chunk is Bill and his family. Another is Chuck. Another is Chuck's former employer. Bill's recent firm is another. We live in *Frag World*, fragments of NOW not connected to anything else.

Frag World is changing as fast as it fragments—as fast as the way people live is detaching itself from the culture of their past.

When a marriage is dissolved by a court—on a certain day it's "over." The people are no longer married as far as the law is concerned.

The marriage between our society (the lives people live) and *our* culture (traditions of government, law, religion, and custom) is dissolving "bit-by-bit." The marriage between society and culture is like a "common-law-marriage" that people tire of. One day both partners realize it's over and they simply go their own ways. As society and culture split there is one significant new element to the separation: society moves on, and with no people to "own" it, culture simply withers into the pages of books and into museums.

The fragmentation we are experiencing is almost like watching an old barn fall down over many years. First the barn is just not used. Then it's not painted. Then one day a few shingles blow off the roof. The paint starts to peel. A board comes loose from the long wall. After a difficult winter a door hangs partly off one hinge. A couple of winters of heavy snowfalls and the barn leans a little to the east. After years of driving by a particular old barn, I told myself, "They don't ever intend to fix that barn." More winters. More hot, dry summers. More loose boards. A hole in the roof. The barn leans at a crazy angle. A rusty tractor shows through the fallen siding. The barn leans still farther and begins to separate from the old concrete silo which still stands straight and tall—without any top. The barn starts to remind people of the famous Leaning Tower in Italy.

The next few times I drove by the abandoned farm it was dark—but one day I drove by in the daylight and saw a big pile of weathered boards with nails sticking out every which way. The barn had finally succumbed to wind or maybe to the weight of a heavy snowfall. A few more years and the owner drove out from the city and picked the wood apart to use in his new house. He wanted a trendy "weathered look." The barn lives on—wood decoration in a gentrified suburb, and a scrubby patch of weeds surrounds a rusty tractor near an abandoned concrete silo. When did the barn stop being a barn?

When has "our culture" stopped being our culture? When does our "culture" only have meaning to historians?

Are we already divorced from our culture or will the divorce only be *final* when Frag-World is here to stay when no one can recognize what a "culture" is—when there's only "This is how we live right now?"

Will we know for certain when our society has become a "Spastic City?"

Chapter 12

Toward Another Culture

Our NOW society will eventually shape its own culture. Human activity acquires norms and rules—either by formal actions like the writing of religious creeds and civil constitutions or by "unwritten agreements" which people observe most of the time.

NOW society is so new that rules have not taken shape. Rules will collect. Heroes will emerge. New "George Washingtons" and "Abe Lincolns" will become new legends. We will find a new culture. When a new culture emerges, people will be amazed at the contrast between the new NOW culture and the traditional culture which came with the immigrants from Europe.

The social divorce from traditional and Americanized Euro-culture is irreversible. People who describe "social goals" (a "right" to this or that) are using language from a discarded culture. NOW thinking assumes a "right" to whatever someone wants at this moment. The discarded culture assumed that society could protect itself from the random behavior of a few who "broke the law." NOW society has discarded the "rights of the whole." People who espouse "social goals" assume that we can reconcile the shattered marriage between everyday life (society) and a discarded culture with its customs and institutions.

Prior to the emergence of a NOW orientation, there was a tacit, if uneasy, acceptance of one by the other (society and inherited customs and institutions). This tacit mutual acceptance is gone.

Religion and society

Accommodation between society (people's actions) and culture (inherited customs and institutions) was based on writings of philosophers, theologians, and other social thinkers from ancient Rome to the Reformation and Enlightenment.

American society (how American people *live*—especially NOW people) rejects religion and philosophy as bases for our institutions—even though most Americans say they are religious. Where the mutual accommodation of society and institutions was based on religious beliefs, the accommodation is rejected. Violence at abortion clinics represents attempts by "religious" people (religious, not Christian; it is unimaginable that Jesus of Nazareth would bomb clinics or shoot physicians) to forcibly re-impose the accommodation of society and a discarded culture. That approach will not work.

"NOW" is the culmination of a secular development. Because Jesus confronted people with a challenge to respond NOW, there is some Christian legitimacy to a type of NOW orientation. However, even when NOW people become Christians, their NOW lives are still not commensurate with the rejected "culture." Whatever remains of cultural accommodation in America is thoroughly secular.

Rejection of religious grounding for our culture stems from our unyielding separation of church and state. We have achieved what the Soviets sought so hard to do—we have isolated the church and Christian thought from everyday life, especially in the public sphere. It may seem strange that this happened, but this is the way it is.

Thus, whether people are modern pagans or modern Christians, our cultural institutions *do not relate* to their lives. Those who are modern pagans reject culturally imposed restraints. Those who are NOW Christians are distant from both secular society and culture. [We will discuss Christianity and NOW society in another book.]

Much of the frustration within organized churches is related to the agendas of many leaders and some supporters who are trying to repair what cannot be repaired.

NOW people may confront our moribund culture, not to restore the fractured "social marriage," but to persuade dying cultural institutions to *listen* to the voices of NOW—for the sake of a *workable* society. Institutional alertness to the concerns of society might forestall social chaos. [Jesus of Nazareth once said, "Render unto Caesar what is Caesar's." Quite clearly, Jesus did not seek secular collapse.]

Cultural dissonance

While some aspects of the rejected culture survive in our social context, there is a dangerous "cultural dissonance" between formal remnants of culture and the way we live. Overlooking this increasing dissonance is not an option.

Norms are ignored at an increasing rate. If this book were accompanied by documentation in newspaper clippings alone, the book would be delivered on a fork lift. Murders are committed for reasons that would be ludicrous, if not so tragic. At the first writing of this paragraph three men under 20 were arraigned locally for a baseball bat beating murder of a friend. According to local news sources, the deceased was the best friend of one of the people who killed him. The triggering event? The deceased reportedly stole a hairpiece from the girl friend of one of the three who killed him. Apparently, this event did not center on three frequently-cited triggers for violence: drugs, racial tension (all parties were Caucasian), or gangs. In this event, there was no discernible link between behavior and inherited cultural norms. The behavior was simply impulse-driven.

A new business reality

No one, and no group can "tell" NOW people to "come back" to traditional norms. The old norms are psychologically unintelligible to NOW people. People cannot "come back" to where they have never been.

With culture in retreat and firms increasingly staffed by NOW people, the business world finds that it pays to accommodate NOW people. Business learns that not everything about traditional practice is indispensable.

Cultural institutions are not as flexible as individual businesses, because culture "belongs to everyone." More and more of the younger "owners" of culture don't want the formal culture. By default, the culture increasingly belongs to older people. Businesses, even our largest firms, are more adaptable than other types of institutions. Businesses are part of society, not of culture. Moreover, competition has forced even giant firms to remain nimble. Companies which adjust to NOW living are more successful than firms locked into the receding culture, especially as success is measured by Wall Street.

Society has forced adjustment of inherited norms and laws:

1. Millions of users of illegal substances have never been prosecuted, though laws regarding these practices are still formally in effect.
2. Laws governing "public propriety" across a broad range of behaviors have been rendered ineffective through changing social behaviors. Nominally, some of these laws (for example, laws governing desecration of the flag) have been neutralized on the basis of first amendment or other grounds. In practice, social behaviors attack laws until a *socially* tolerable way of neutralizing the laws is found.

Interestingly, First Amendment rights cannot be used to justify use of certain epithets because *society* does not choose to apply the "higher" first amendment protection to these forms of speech. There is no "rightness or wrongness" to behaviors which society protects or attacks.

Instead, through high profile events, society collides with inherited norms and effectively dictates changes in the norms.

Culture has yielded to society. However, many businesses and institutions could not function effectively if norms were swept away too rapidly.

If the "owners" of the culture deferred completely to social behavior, the institutions of the dying culture would disappear and nothing would restrain social behavior except countervailing social behavior. This scenario would foster open warfare among subgroups of society.

For example, shoplifting is common, though it is illegal. A certain level of enforcement is necessary or one of two outcomes would occur: 1. Businesses would lose so much money that they would disappear and the services or goods they provide would be lost; 2. Businesses would enforce their own "laws" to survive.

With no enforcement of existing laws, customers and businesses would operate like enemy camps and their low level "warfare" would undermine all social functioning.

Because they fear social warfare, "owners" of the culture essentially "demand" that NOW people adhere to some inherited norms. This "demand" is hollow, in part because exceptions highlight the incongruity between the broader "society" and the "formal culture." Partial conformity with cultural "demands" is enforced at great cost in both money spent and lives torn apart.

Consider the relationship between non-conforming people and institutions, especially schools. Many non-conforming students (often NOW people) are in a running conflict with school administrators. These students inhibit the learning process for other students at great cost to society because educational attainment by all students is needed if our country is to compete in an increasingly high-tech global business environment.

Generally, the non-conformers pay an even greater price in their own lost educational opportunity because they are frequently removed from schools as a disciplinary measure. They are educationally handicapped because they do not develop skills demanded in a high-tech economy. They become a financial burden on society and their lives are torn apart through intermittent clashes with institutions.

If society fragments and moves away from its business enterprises, our standard of living will decline, and society will be angry about "what we have lost." This anger would surface as generalized rage because specific causes of the "loss" could not be identified.

The new owners of culture

A culture disappears unless someone or some group chooses to "own" the culture.

Many younger Americans who would inherit our formal culture [norms and institutions] do not *want* to own the culture because they are NOW people and the formal culture is rooted in the paradigms of continuous time, which is not part of their world.

At the same time, most Americans are dependent on an orderly society which brings them food, electrical service, medical care, a monetary system, and safe water—to name a few things. In the absence of functioning institutions, these things disappear. The former Soviet Union provides some evidence of the kind of struggle to be faced when a formal culture is rejected by its owners. It becomes difficult to provide services and goods which were once taken for granted.

The new owners of America (younger people) will struggle with these issues. They (or their spokespersons) will confront this issue: "Do *we* [NOW people] change or do we scrap our culture and lose the lifestyle we like?"

Some NOW people are analysts in their work and NOW people in their personal lives. *These* people who straddle two orientations toward time will be significant spokespersons for the NOW orientation in the struggle over a new culture.

We believe that both society AND cultural norms and institutions will change and that this "mutual" movement charts the course most likely to bring a new and stable formal culture in America. *If* this occurs, the new "society" will be different from the society of the early part of the 21st century, *and* its "formal culture" will also be different from the unravelling residual culture which entered the early 21st century.

We noted that the formal culture has lost the ability to "demand" that society conform to the once-dominant culture. Society has changed too much and many people, especially NOW people, simply do not understand the traditional culture, and yet NOW people may want to avoid the instability which would result from discarding the shell of our formal culture.

Business accommodates its new reality

1. Employers Relax the Rules

A New Business Reality in America has already begun to accommodate the New Worker of the new century—the NOW worker. Rules are more flexible. Departures from "expected" behavior are often overlooked. The long-range "unwritten contract" between worker and employer is gone.

This accommodation provides employers with a broader labor pool and gives employees a greater range of potential employers. This new accommodation has also resulted in higher labor turnover (a cost to employers) and lower wages (a cost to employees) and less job stability (also a cost to employees).

The accommodation has given younger employees the freedom to be NOW people and to remain in the labor force.

If an employer insisted on "traditional" behavioral norms, the employer would encounter serious labor trouble, though in a few cases such as old-line firms cultivating a traditional image, a strong behavioral code might prevail. Even in this setting, a star performer may be able to opt out of traditional behavioral norms.

2. Employees Learn about the Formal Culture

Contract law and the ability of a business to obtain funds for operations depend on staying within the bounds of the moribund formal culture.

A business has "sunk costs" which must be recovered or the business will not survive. The business must honor contracts, repay loans, and deliver an acceptable product at a reasonable cost or it will not survive. A New Worker will understand the employer's obligation to honor contracts and pay debts or the worker will be of no value to the employer.

Contracts and debt repayment are not part of the NOW orientation, but working within these legal restraints is a "bare minimum" requirement for NOW people or their employer will not survive and their wages may disappear. As NOW people encounter these "bare minimums," they bump into limits on living by impulse. A small segment of the NOW population avoids even these modest limits and stays outside of norms by engaging in unlawful behaviors to support their lifestyle or by living outside the visible economy.

3. Mutual Accommodation Is Workable

The key thrust of this book is our belief that a social divorce has taken place: Society—especially the large, younger segment of society consisting of NOW oriented people and many analytically-oriented people—has divorced the inherited formal culture.

Following society's *escape from time*, a new question is raised, "Quo vadis?" "Where do we go from here?"

When/if the "owners" of culture (in general, older people) acknowledge that the "social contract" which once existed is *gone*, remaining elements of the formal culture could become sufficiently pliable to be a bridge to a new NOW culture.

NOW people have made it clear that they do not like the world as it is. If they also decide that they do not like what they think will happen next, they will foster a culture which fits their NOW orientation.

As long as NOW people think that the current "owners" of the culture are the problem, the social divorce will taste bitter.

As long as current "owners" of the culture exclude NOW oriented people as co-owners, the aftermath of the social divorce will worsen.

America has been moving toward a social divorce for years—perhaps beginning in the 1960s, perhaps in the 1970s, perhaps decades earlier—but we have never defined the problem. When a problem is fuzzy and poorly understood, there is no meaningful progress toward a solution.

We wrote this book to name the phenomenon—a social disconnect (divorce) is occurring in America.

New culture

NOW people will not initiate a movement toward a culture they view as irrelevant.

The formal culture is entirely outside the day to day world of many NOW people. Not only is formal culture not relevant to NOW people—it does not even exist for them, except as an occasional threat or enemy when institutions enforce laws. NOW people act on impulse, and laws are often experienced as an after-the-fact surprise—as a "trick" played on impulse actors by a system which, psychologically, is divorced from their lives.

Some steps could lead to temporary accommodation of the residual formal culture to society, especially NOW society. The first steps can best be taken by institutions and "owners" of the residual formal culture. Some would say "the establishment" is the owner, but that is not really the case. Many "establishment" people are young NOW people. It is more appropriate to say that the residual formal culture belongs to traditional people, whatever their age and whatever their wealth or relationship to the so-called "establishment."

Why should institutions and "owners" of the formal culture act?

1. NOW people are younger and their orientation as well as their age does not provide them the insight to see the high costs of continuous quarreling following a social divorce. NOW people

will not seek rapprochement with residual institutions because the basis for those institutions is not relevant to them.

2. The costs of the ever-widening social divorce will grow until society cannot pay the costs. If another formal culture does not emerge to guide a large and growing block of NOW people, breakdown of the unwritten "social contract" will be followed by general social breakdown. It is impossible to predict what might occur, but likely scenarios include social unrest or even chaos.

Direct incorporation of NOW views into dying cultural norms and institutions is not possible for at least two reasons:

a. "Owners of the culture" will simply not accept this course of action.

b. "Culture" cannot be decreed or developed by fiat. Dictatorships (notably the Soviet dictatorship under Stalin, and also the government of the Directorate in revolutionary France) tried to impose a culture, but these attempts did not work. The French Revolution crumbled quickly and the Soviet system evolved into a police state in which the "culture" was "borne" by the people as a burden preferable to Siberia or death.

We will look for ways to build another culture which is a superset of the old—even while recognizing that the old and dying culture is being reconfigured by changes in society. The society is reconfiguring more rapidly than the remnants of the old culture can evolve, suggesting that creative cultural intervention may be the only way to shape congruity between culture and society without societal chaos.

Focal actors

If there is a creative re-shaping of institutional culture (including laws and a set of norms for living), the focal actors will be from among people between 30 and 55. Many in this group focus on prosperity—not merely while they are employed, but when they retire. They are driven by a state of mind, largely inherited from the previous generation, a state of mind that focuses on avoidance of hopelessness experienced in America during the "Great Depression" of the 1930s and experienced through much of the world after two world wars.

The group from 30 to 55 (essentially the Baby Boomers) is very work focused. Nevertheless, these people would like to take time to think deeply. Their work-focus has kept them from thinking deeply about things beyond their job. The attraction of many of these people to fundamentalist religion is linked to their desire for answers to basic questions. They have focused heavily on their careers, leaving inadequate time for reflection on religious or philosophical questions.

We suggest how a new culture will be born. The old paradigm (the intertwined "American" culture and "American" society, the "American" way of life) is crumbling but the new is now being born. The new will have a greatly changed shape.

1. Many old institutions will die (perhaps classical music, perhaps classical theater, various organizations reflecting the immigrant society or the small-town aspects of America). Whole groupings of institutions will die as the corner store, corner gas station and corner tavern have been dying for some time.

2. New institutions will emerge—business will become a major subculture, perhaps the focus of culture, not because this is "right," but because this falls on our current path of change. People will work but many may almost not know why—only to fund what comes next or to eroticize success. Success may also be interpreted as doing/having/being. Recognition Societies will re-emerge as "reincarnations" of lodges. "Purchased" recognition will increase.

Whereas people formerly donated buildings to colleges to "immortalize" their names, their counterparts will build recognition through what they DO, what they HAVE, and who they supposedly ARE. Status possessions, status vacations, status offices, status awards will be ever more sought. Status knows no bounds, but in groups such as gangs, the road to status may be very different than in, for example, fundamentalist groups.

If you hate the emergence of NOW society, adapt and adjust. It's what's happening. No one can control NOW society because it's coming from the bottom up, from the young toward the older. One generation, two generations—being eased aside by what's happening—whether the older generations like it or not.

Marketers and industrial leaders design tactics and products. States, cities, and the federal government create programs. The longer a program takes to test, the farther it is from what's happening. The longer a product takes to design, the more likely it loses tons of money. Marketers are faster to adapt. Marketers can get there almost as fast as NOW society gets where it's going to be next.

Whoever plans for what's next is more likely to succeed if the focus is on NOW, more likely to fail if the program is long-term. These are the measures used by Wall Street.

Long-term projects to manage how people live create social nightmares—housing initiatives become slums; free rides create cycles of poverty; arming the defenseless creates aggressors. When people feel someone else is doing something *to* them or *for* them, they reject what is done *to* them, and they choose their own way of shaping what is done *for* them.

People become involved in something done *with* them—local projects done with their consent, education programs, a do-it-yourself (with help) project like Habitat for Humanity.

NOW people are not more or less human than people locked in a pattern of past, present, and future, not fundamentally different from analytical people. But their mindset is very different.

NOW people reject the pattern of life they think has left their parents and grandparents without a life and left their generation with more problems than any other generation.

"So, what's new?," an analyst might ask. Everything is new. NOW people and NOW images of life are not *yet* dominant, but NOW ways of thinking and living are popping up everywhere—too often not recognized as expression of an emerging society. The conflagration in Waco, Texas was seen as the government against people on the fringe. Then came the terrible bombing in Oklahoma City. That was a different "fringe" event. The line between "fringe" and "new way" blurs as "fringe" activities occur in more and more places—post office shootings, business place shootings, high school shootings, grade school shootings.

"NOW thinking" gives people an action orientation. Creative dissatisfaction does not guarantee "good" results. It may only guarantee "results." Dissonance between NOW society and "conventional" society widens the already huge gap between NOW people and conventional society. No amount of prison expansion can contain people whose NOW behavior clashes with laws representing a passing era. The dissonance between NOW society and "conventional" society is amplified by perceived differences in dealing with "unwanted" or "unconventional" behaviors. As of the date of this writing a radio report told of the "largest pyramid scheme in American history." The report indicated that the man involved had defrauded thousands of would-be investors of $700 million and that the accused man could receive up to twenty years in prison. On a smaller scale an occasional "armed robbery" is conducted by a person carrying a look-alike toy pistol. It's not impossible that the accused robber toting a toy pistol may have stolen less than $100 but could also receive a sentence of up to twenty years. Even though NOW people are not analysts, it does not require analysis to recognize the similar treatment of the major "swindler" and the petty "robber" as incongruous and "illogical." The "irrational" behavior of conventional society in dealing with the swindler and the robber further spreads the gap between NOW people and "conventional" culture.

NOW society and "action orientation" are two sides of one coin. Action orientation legitimizes NOW actions and a NOW orientation is inherent in NOW thought.

Action orientation did not "cause" the conflagration at the Branch Davidian compound in Waco, didn't cause the bombing in Oklahoma City, did not cause a wave of workplace or school shootings, did not cause cult suicides in Switzerland and Los Angeles. Still, there is a link between NOW thought and a rapid increase in "illogical or "irrational" acts.

Some things are done *because* they are not rational. Many NOW acts directly reject analytical culture and its precursor—a culture of past-present-future.

Those two older cultural types attempt to dominate our increasingly NOW society. Both of those cultural types are rejected as undermining "life"—as making "real life" impossible to enjoy.

Both analytical culture and past-present-future, time-bound culture are experienced as ways to limit "life, liberty and the pursuit of happiness."

NOW society wants as few limits as possible. No limits at all would be best. Limits are defined at the point of pain. Pain can be financial social, physical.

NOW living stretches financial boundaries with record numbers of bankruptcies. NOW living accepts no social limits. If social limits seem to be forming, NOW people fight back. Workplace murders, drive-by shootings, school massacres are expressions by people who are rejected in some way and who act out their feelings of, "*No* way is this going to happen to me."

Physical limits are overcome by doing an "end run" around limits. Wealthy men physically unable to compete buy professional sports franchises. Other people identify with famous sports figures. Consider how many shirts and jerseys are seen everywhere in America—people wear names and uniform numbers of superb athletes to do an end run around their own physical limitations and their anonymity.

NOW society is outrunning the cultural structures of analytical culture and time-bound culture.

NOW people introduced business into the Internet so rapidly that Internet practice outdistanced laws and business structures. The Internet leaves legal and business structures gasping to understand even *whether* the Internet can be managed. Outmoded business structures simply don't compete on the Internet.

On the Internet, NOW is king. The Internet created a class of billionaires in the 1990s—billionaires under 30 years old. There are more billionaires under forty than all the billionaires in America when the first NOW billionaires were born.

Is a NOW approach to business a quick path to wealth? No guarantee, but in accelerating markets "slow and easy" is like an e-ticket to the wrong destination.

NOW society creates its own "wow" factor. One day a person thinks of society through the old paradigms—analyzing the flow of time through past-present-future. Then, somehow, in a quick shiver of recognition, that person sees NOW people all around and knows: old frameworks are gone. Their shells are still around, but the people have moved on. Those ways of living are dead.

You might think, "Not true. There are analysts and time-flow people everywhere I look." You can "prove" your point.

You'd be correct to think that—and you'd also be fooling yourself. I live in Wisconsin. I love to walk through the woods and grassy fields on a sunny day in October. For a moment it feels like mid-summer. Butterflies, flies, a few bees buzzing around. But it's not summer. An occasional swirl of wind reminds me that a stronger wind will soon scream through. Rain will come, mixing with wet snow, and then the fields will be white.

NOW society is a wind of change. Not to notice the NOW world is to think the old aspects of culture are supreme. The old ways are quivering golden leaves on the aspens, glorious in the fall sunshine; and soon to be piled up in rows against the fences or in the gullies.

Laws, customs, music, art, religious thought—whatever represents the old cultural dominance, all dying—or dead—glistening in the sunshine of change and soon gone entirely.

NOW society will have new rules, new laws, new customs, new music, changed art, and changed religion.

"Wait for me!" Don't shout "Wait!" Ask a question, a new question. "Where do I get aboard?"

You are not on the Titanic any more. You're in a lifeboat. It's that sudden. Walk where the NOW people walk. Shop where NOW people shop. Listen to NOW music.

How useful are the old ways? Look at the prison budgets.

How useless are old customs? Watch a twenty-year old movie; watch a TV program from the 1980s.

Music? Art? Listen! Look! Touch!

Religious thought? Old-time religion—a sentimental journey.

Logical theology? No one cares? Appeal to authority? Not in America.

Creative Dissatisfaction fuels NOW society. Dissatisfaction does not describe a theme. The driving motive of NOW society is to be *other* than analytical, *other* than locked in an orderly flow of time. When NOW society creates its own culture, it will be something not seen before. NOW culture will spring from dozens of fragments of what people do.

If history books give a clue to what kind of culture will grow out of NOW society, it's this: bits and pieces will be recognizable to somebody. If there are any analytical thinkers to examine NOW culture, they will theorize about how things came together. A pattern of rejection is not an outline for the new.

Our thoughts about NOW culture are disjointed. Why? Because we think about small bits of turbulence while NOW culture is still emerging.

NOW society is not tuned to categories of good or bad from the "once upon a time" culture of past-present-future and not tuned to the utilitarian culture of analysts—parents and grandparents of NOW people.

NOW society will have its own culture. It will give birth to something new.

It will give birth to a culture which authenticates transactional behavior, i.e., if you and I agree on a behavior, it's "good."

The new culture will validate social niches apart from any coherent whole.

In contrast to the culture we are discarding, religions will proliferate, splintering into: leader-driven cults, special-revelation religions, totally secular "religions," created to achieve secular goals or to validate selected behaviors. Where the Christian faith at one time interpenetrated the society, there will be no link to an "accepted religion."

NOW culture will reflect a "referendum mentality"—with a majority vote, anything is "cultural."

As society moves spastically with no center and no coherent "whole," there will be no identifiable "owners" of culture. The arts, humanities and literature will "float" ownerless, like loose items in an orbiting spacecraft in zero gravity.

The collective memory of "what is enduring" will be blotted out even as the ability to "remember" more through mass storage media grows. Instead of "An American Heritage" or "The Heritage of Civilization," NOW society will bring along in disarray "whatever is available." The possibilities are too many to enumerate.

The author once attended a potluck meal at which half of all the "courses" were chocolate cakes. In a similar, unbalanced way, NOW society will "remember" more than anyone wants to know about some of its potential culture and may "forget" what made it distinct.

The character and irony of NOW culture will be shaped by a fragmented social memory, held in disassociated social niches. Some day,

NOW living will end. When people wake up following the end of the NOW party, it will be THEN.

People who live "THEN," when NOW society is gone, will be unable to know the real character of NOW, because our fragmented culture will be unreadable in a coherent way. NOW society will be the best-documented society in history, and yet it will be opaque to an outsider who tries to understand its "soul."

This will be the legacy of NOW when it becomes THEN.